2022

Miami & South Beach

The Restaurant Enthusiast's Discriminating Guide

Andrew Delaplaine

*Andrew Delaplaine is the Food Enthusiast.
When he's not playing tennis,
he dines anonymously
at the Publisher's (considerable) expense.*

James Cubby – Senior Editor

The Restaurant Enthusiast's
Discriminating Guide

Table of Contents

INTRODUCTION

By Way of Introduction – Why Miami? Transportation & Tips for Getting Around - Parking Headaches - If Your Car Is Towed - The Best Cab Company - Specific Information During Your Visit - Visitors' Centers

BY WAY OF INTRODUCTION

Food, Wine & Travel

I've written about food, wine and travel for decades, and while I've lived on South Beach since the late-1980s, most of the writing about food and wine had to do with New York or London or Paris, definitely *not* South Beach. One could write endless "travel" pieces about Miami, but the "food" and "wine" offerings were pretty much limited unless you went to **Joe's Stone Crab** for the food and **The Forge** for the wine.

My, my ... how things have changed.

Miami and South Beach are now year-round destinations. The nightlife industry, the fuel that drives the engine, churns all through the summer, never letting up. Most of the top bars and clubs have licenses that permit them to remain open selling liquor till 5am.

As a butler I once had in London used to say: *Raathuur!*

Chefs from all over the world have established outposts on South Beach, eager to be part of the scene.

Boutique hotels (the **W**, the **Setai**, the **Gale**, etc.) have flooded in and cranked up the quality of service to the 4- and even 5-Star levels. (Trust me, child, it wasn't always like this.)

This really is a world-class town. And in this book I will share some things I like about it (and a few I don't.) This is not a book to tell you how to get from your hometown to Miami International Airport, or from MIA to South Beach. You can figure that out by yourself. (And if you can't, stay home.)

It's also *not a comprehensive book* covering the County. It's not a phone book or something purporting to cover everything. God forbid. Who'd want to read such a book? No. This, like my other *Guides*, is my *personal* take on the scene for visitors, not necessarily residents. Thus, there are no listings for some of the great restaurants I've trekked to in South and West Miami. The listings are intentionally brief, so they can be digested fast.

WHY MIAMI?

Because it may be the most *interesting* city in the U.S. There are probably only a handful of cities in America that offer truly distinctive "feels," and by that I mean a unique sensation you get when you're there that you don't get anywhere else.

Boston has it, Charleston has it, New York, San Francisco, New Orleans, Chicago, Vegas and a handful of other cities large and small have it. But, to be honest, if you removed my blindfold on a street in Buffalo or Cleveland, I'd have a hard time telling them apart at first glance. (Or even second glance.)

Not so Miami.

And it's not all sex, drugs and rock 'n roll. (Well ... it's not, really.) It's home to some major league cultural institutions, from the **Miami City Ballet** headed by Edward Villella; the **New World Symphony** with topper Michael Tilson Thomas, the stupendously successful **Art**

Basel. The off-the-wall collection of tens of thousands of items of decorative and propaganda art assembled by Mickey Wolfson in his **Wolfsonian Museum** now operated by FIU is worth a trip to Miami all by itself. As is the **South Beach Wine & Food Festival** pushed to the top of the heap in its category by the relentless energy of **Lee Brian Schrager.** Schrager and the others have an infectious optimism that has transformed small start-ups into world-class institutions that have made lasting contributions in their fields.

As a young city, these institutions were founded and nurtured by strong-willed individuals. And built from the ground up. If they began with something to prove, they proved it.

But I'm assuming you know why you're coming here. I'm not here to sell you on the town. If it's February, it's probably got a lot more to do with a suntan than with Schumann, and you're probably more interested in a good mojito than Mozart. And you might not care or even know the difference between a Degas and a Duchamp, a Picasso and a Pissarro. And maybe you *are* here because of the sex, drugs and rock 'n roll. Whatever.

Let's face it: how many towns in America let their clubs, bars and dives stay open till 5am selling booze? (And everything else—they don't call it Sodom by the Sea for nuttin'!)

Miami has an edge. And the edge is what's most interesting about it, with the hundred different ethnic influences all mixing together to make it so dramatic, Mozart and the ballet notwithstanding.

GETTING ABOUT

AIRPORT FLYER

http://www.miamidade.gov/transit/routes_detail.asp?route=150

One of the most economical ways to get to the Miami Airport is to take the Airport Flyer, an express bus with service between MIA, Metrorail, and Miami Beach that costs only a few dollars. The Airport Flyer runs every half hour from 6 a.m. to 11 p.m. Look for the Airport Flyer signs at bus stops.

SOUTH BEACH LOCAL BUS

This local shuttle service is the cheapest way to get around South Beach. It stops every 10 or 15 minutes at numerous corners. It's air-conditioned and only costs 25 cents. (You'll see signs posted everywhere.) Personally, I use Uber to get around, but if I needed to or had a budget, I'd use this service religiously.

MIAMI HOP-ON HOP-OFF BUS

https://city-sightseeing.com

Visitors to Miami can travel all over Miami and learn about the city at the same time on one of the many red double-decker Hop-On Hop-Off Buses. Buses travel to Downtown Miami, the Design District, Coconut Grove, Coral Gables and beyond. A two-day pass costs $39 allowing you to hop on and hop off at any stop as many times as you wish. For schedules and list of stops.

BIKES

MIAMI HOP-ON HOP-OFF BUS

https://city-sightseeing.com

Visitors to Miami can travel all over Miami and learn about the city at the same time on one of the many red double-decker Hop-On Hop-Off Buses. Buses travel to Downtown Miami, the Design District, Coconut Grove, Coral Gables and beyond. A two-day pass costs $39 allowing you to hop on and hop off at any stop as many times as you wish. For schedules and list of stops.

BIKES

https://citibikemiami.com

Since most of South Beach is located within one square mile you'll see locals getting around by skateboard and bicycles. Biking is a viable means of transportation in Miami Beach and there are bicycle stands all over the beach and many well-marked bike lanes. Citi bike, a popular bike sharing system that has partnered with the City of Miami Beach, offers approximately 1,000 bikes accessible from 100 stations located throughout Miami Beach. This system allows renters to pick up a bike (a charge card is needed) and the bike can be returned to any of the 100 stations located throughout Miami Beach.

RENTING A CAR? THINK TWICE

We recommend you rent a car only if you're planning on leaving South Beach a lot. Parking is a never-ending hassle, the City writes tickets relentlessly and ruthlessly and just finding parking spots on the weekends is a major pain in the ass.

Since South Beach is so small, we suggest you leave your car parked securely in a city-owned garage and either walk or take short Uber / Lyft rides. Even if you use the valet service when you go to a fancy hotel for a drink, the valet will cost you between $30 and $40.

The valets at restaurants are often *not* a real convenience. When it's busy, it can take quite a bit of time for the valet to retrieve your car. So best advice: Uber / Lyft it everywhere. I live here, and I do.

IF YOUR CAR IS TOWED

And trust me, it *will* be towed if you park in a tow away zone. Towing is a cottage industry in this town. The problem: you won't notice the signs until it's too late. Some businesses watch the often hard-to-see tow away zones very carefully and spy as you park in what will look like an OK place, but is really a tow away zone, and within seconds of you leaving your car, a call is made and you are towed.

The towing companies (there are two of them that have a monopoly) make hundreds of thousands of dollars each year on unsuspecting tourists. The City even gets a kickback (uh, I'm sorry, an "administrative fee") for each car towed. It's a shame, but it's true. In other towns, a tow truck can be thought of as providing a service. Here, it's a predatory act sanctioned by the City to rip you off. So, you've been warned.

When your car is towed, it won't be far away. It will be over on a little street just a few minutes from Lincoln Road on the way to the Venetian Causeway. When you get back to where you left your car, look for the little green sign (that you didn't notice before) posted on a wall and this sign will tell you which company has your car. Call **Tremont Towing, 305-672-2395**, or **Beach Towing, 305-534-2128**, to find out which one has your car and how much it is (it'll be between $100 and $350, depending on the season). Summon **UBER,** and go get your car. Stop by an ATM machine. The buggers only take cash, of course.

Speaking of **UBER**. The absolute best way to enjoy South Beach if you are driving over in your own car or a rental is to park the car in a garage (like the one centrally located just north of Lincoln Road on 17th Street), leave it there and take **UBER.** This is what I do. I leave my car parked in front of my house, especially after 6 or 7 in the evening when it's hard to find a good space and then I take UBER all over town.

You'll ride in nicer cars for cheaper fares and there's no tipping. If you don't have the Uber app, download it now on your smartphone and use my code when you sign up and get a couple of free rides. Code is – **Andrewd145**

THE BEST CAB COMPANY (There Isn't One)
Central Cab – 305-532-5555 – is a company based on South Beach, so their drivers always know the best route to take you anywhere. It's not the "best" cab company. It's the "only" cab company. I haven't used these old, smelly beat-up cabs in years, not since **Uber / Lyft** got started. Everywhere you're going is only five or six minutes away on the island. Use my Uber code if you do not have the app and you'll get a couple of free rides. Cheaper than a cab by far. Code is – **Andrewd145**

SPECIFIC INFO DURING YOUR VISIT
Check out the listings in the weekly newspaper New Times, which has boxes on every corner, or use your laptop (or increasingly these days, even your cell phone) and go to their web site, www.miaminewtimes.com. The Miami Herald only has a good list in its Friday edition. But they also have comprehensive listings online at www.miamiherald.com.

VISITORS' CENTERS

THE ART DECO WELCOME CENTER
1001 Ocean Drive, Miami Beach, (10th and Ocean), 305-763-8026
www.mdpl.org/welcome-center/visitors-center/
Located on Ocean Drive across from the beach, the Art Deco Welcome Center offers visitors a center for

information, tours, and a gift shop filled with Miami Beach memorabilia and souvenirs as well as Art Deco gifts and books.

ART DECO TOURS

Learn all about South Beach's historical Art Deco District in a VIP Art Deco Walking Tour. Transport in time back to the 20's, 30's and beyond. Learn about the colorful history and admire unique architecture and design with exclusive access to interiors and rooftops. Elevate the experience with the Art Deco Cocktail tour. For schedule and rates, visit www.artdecotours.com or call 305-814-4058.

MIAMI BEACH VISITORS' CENTER (MBVC) AT THE CONVENTION CENTER

530 17TH ST, Miami Beach. 305-672-1270. Daily from 10-4.

WEB: www.miamibeachguest.com. **WEBSITE DOWN AT PRESSTIME**

This state-of-the-art facility offers a multilingual staff along with tourist, business and residential amenities. Their literature rack holds over 200 brochures, magazines, newspapers and maps, calendar of events and visitors' guides full of helpful facts. They offer on-the-spot hotel accommodations, and **20 daily tour excursions.** They are the official distributor of Miami's best attraction pass, the Go Miami Card. They provide the MB chamber of commerce's newest feature, the In Card, which offers tourists and residents money-saving amenities at local businesses. Hotel reservations: 800-666-4519.

The A to Z Listings

Ridiculously Extravagant
Sensible Alternatives
Quality Bargain Spots

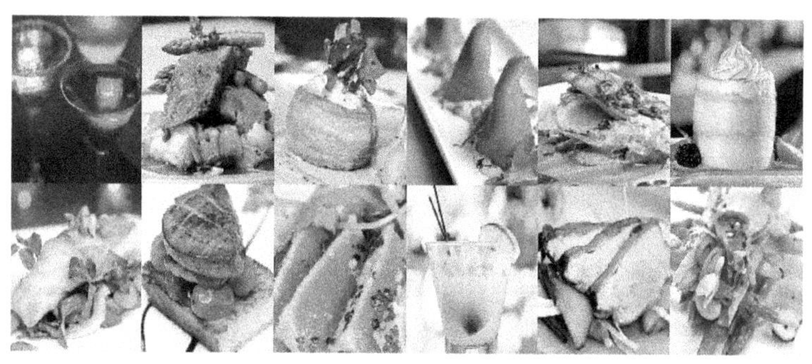

INTRODUCTION
Miami-Dade Food Tours
SOUTH BEACH
(Ridiculously Extravagant - Sensible Alternatives - Quality Bargain Spots)
MIDDLE & NORTH BEACHES
(Bal Harbour, Surfside) **MIAMI NORTH**
DESIGN DISTRICT-MIDTOWN-BISCAYNE CORRIDOR
DOWNTOWN-BRICKELL
LITTLE HAVAVA
CORAL GABLES
COCONUT GROVE
KEY BISCAYNE

INTRODUCTION

The greatest pleasure for me has been to witness firsthand the explosion of culinary diversity that has made Greater Miami one of the most interesting "food towns" in the U.S.

Not to take anything away from New Orleans or Charleston or Savannah or any other locale in America that boasts a distinctive cuisine, but I can safely say Miami's offerings are terribly more interesting and culturally engaging than any town in the U.S. besides New York.

Why?

Because the cuisines in New Orleans and places like Baltimore—while among the best America has to offer—are generally quite static. Sorry, folks, but in the end, shrimp and grits are still shrimp and grits. That soft-shelled crab at that little shack on the Chesapeake—it's the same year in and year out.

But when was the last time you went to a restaurant and had Guatemalan food? Or Peruvian.

All right—I admit the cuisines you can expect to find in Miami will have a Latin slant—but what's wrong with that? You'll find such a huge variety of cuisines you've never tried before. You'll travel a long, long way from the black beans and rice of a Cuban meal to a ceviche made by a Peruvian.

The excitement generated by the nightlife industry, climate and cultural diversity one gets in Miami has attracted a Who's Who of famous international chefs. The unqualified success of the **Food Network South Beach Wine & Food Festival** (directly attributable to the obsessive single-mindedness of **Lee Brian Schrager** of **Southern Wine & Spirits**) brought chefs from all over the world to South Beach. Many who came, saw what they liked, and opened outposts in their global empires here on the sandy shores of the Billion Dollar Sandbar.

But a big name in France or New York is no guarantee of success. **David Bouley's** aptly named "Evolution" in the Ritz-Carlton might have easily been named "Natural Selection" because it closed within a year. South Beach is as tough a town as New York or anywhere else where the public is fickle and the rents are as sky high as a chef's ambition.

But the good news is that there seems to be a new opening every week.

MIAMI-DADE FOOD TOURS

If you don't want to do your homework, consider following a guide as you tour the area. I've done a couple of these and they're really quite fun.

MIAMI CULINARY TOURS
LOCATIONS: Little Havana, South Beach, Miami City
Tours: 786-942-8856
www.miamiculinarytours.com
COST: Rates vary by season (special rates for children, military)

FOOD TOURS OF MIAMI
LOCATIONS: Coral Gables and South Beach
www.foodtoursofmiami.com and
www.pubcrawlofmiami.com
COST: Rates vary by season (special rates for children, military)

SOUTH BEACH

Ridiculously Extravagant
Sensible Alternatives
Quality Bargain Spots

APPLE A DAY
1534 Alton Rd, 305-538-4569
www.appleadaymiami.com
WEBSITE DOWN AT PRESSTIME
CUISINE: Juice bar/Smoothies
DRINKS: No Booze
SERVING: 8 a.m. – 10 p.m.
PRICE RANGE: $$
Health food market offering usual health food items plus fresh juices, salads, and wraps. Favorites: Vegan pizza and variety of tacos. Raw vitamins and supplements. Counter-service with seating indoors & out.

AURA AT BOOKS & BOOKS
927 Lincoln Rd.; 305-695-8898
No web site
CUISINE: Contemporary, Eclectic; some good Cuban
DRINKS: Beer & Wine
SERVING: Breakfast, lunch and dinner daily
Take a minute to look up at the historic Sterling Building in which this café is housed. It's one of the best examples of "Streamline Moderne" Art Deco architecture in the country. I used to have an office in this building and loved walking to work there every day. Excellent spot for breakfast, lunch or dinner on Lincoln Road, which you may consider a big fat Tourist Trap with a bunch of overpriced eateries with boring food served indifferently. That's not true in this place.

AZABU
Marriott Stanton South Beach
161 Ocean Dr, Miami Beach, 786-276-0520
https://azabuglobal.com
CUISINE: Sushi/Japanese
DRINKS: Full bar
SERVING: Dinner only
PRICE RANGE: $$$$
NEIGHBORHOOD: SoFi (South of Fifth)
Tucked away off the lobby of this waterfront Marriott is an upscale eatery with a fixed price menu featuring an open kitchen and bar are. The light stained wood paneling looks striking because it is mounted horizontally, and matches the light color of the wooden bar where you sit in the Den and look on while the chefs work creating your meal. Clean, pristine, Spartan surroundings. Very efficient service (not something we're terribly used to on casual South Beach). The lighting is very cleverly designed, with pin spots in one place and recessed lighting elsewhere, all very romantic. The Robata Bar is completely different, with the countertop where you sit dominated by a busy swirling marble design. There's a beautiful shellfish display when you walk in—all the raw food that will soon be your dinner. Expect to sit for 2 hours. Great sushi offerings including Japanese barracuda, Tuna kama, and Tempura Whole Squid. The place is not cheap, so if you're on a budget, take advantage of their Happy Hour 6-8 p.m.

BAOLI
1908 Collins Ave., Miami Beach, 305-674-8822
www.baoli-group.com
CUISINE: French, Italian
DRINKS: Full Bar
SERVING: Dinner
PRICE RANGE: $$$$

As good as the food is, the best thing about Baoli is the charming patio-courtyard with a canopy of shade trees sprinkled with lights that give the place an other-worldly feel. A big menu covers all the bases, from a raw bar to sushi to a great selection of pastas (black truffle risotto) to grilled items (an 18oz grilled rib eye), to seafood (get the bouillabaisse). Oh, that "other-worldly" feel? You'll come back to this world when they bring you the check.

BARTON G: THE RESTAURANT
1427 West Ave.; 305-672-8881
www.bartongtherestaurant.com
CUISINE: American, Contemporary
DRINKS: Full bar
SERVING: Dinner nightly from 6
PRICE RANGE: $$$$
The expensive (and expensively famous) creation of Barton G. An experience you won't forget. When you come here, throw caution to the wind and surrender yourself. Worth every penny. (I went there on my birthday and ordered a three-pound lobster tail: we were eating lobster salad for two days!)

BAYSIDE GRILL
The Standard Hotel; 40 Island Ave.; 786-245-0880; CUISINE: Greek, Mediterranean, International; DRINKS: Full bar; SERVING: Daily 7am-midnight; WEB: www.standardhotels.com
PRICE RANGE: $$$
There are damn few places where you can have a drink and see Biscayne Bay. (Even on Ocean Drive, the park is between you and the water and you can't see the ocean, either, except way out.) Well, over here on the first island on the Venetian Causeway, you'll find a perfect spot. It's got a pool, a restaurant, a spa. L.A. hotelier Andre Balazs bought the rundown Lido Spa and renovated it into one of

his hip Standard hotels. It's just stunning at sunset by the pool. (The French fries are the best!) Note: there's nowhere to park, so you *have* to valet if you drive. Take an Uber. $$$

BARCELONETA
1400 20th St, Miami Beach, 305-538-9299
http://barcelonetamiami.com
CUISINE: Spanish
DRINKS: Full bar
SERVING: Lunch/Dinner
PRICE RANGE: $$
NEIGHBORHOOD: Sunset Harbour
Popular storefront eatery with a menu of small plates of typical Spanish fare. The name comes from "La Barceloneta," which is the section of Barcelona built in the 18th Century and is home to the big broad beach area of the town. People come here to go to the beach, have fun, eat tapas, you name it. Whenever I'm in Barcelona (which is never too often, as I love the place), I stay in the L'Eixample area, but I never fail to come down to La Barceloneta for some great seafood you find in little spots off the beaten tourist trap. Here on South Beach, it's a little different, but their heart's in the right place. Plenty of outdoor tables as well as a spacious indoor area. A small cozy bar in the corner where you'll find me sitting, drinking and eating when I stop in. Favorites include: Steak tartar and Spicy shrimp. Great wine selection. Great casual dining environment. (The marina is just across the street, so you'll find people from the boats docked there dropping in here all the time—they come from all over the world, so you never know who you'll meet.) The food's not *quite* as good as it is in La Barceloneta, but, hey, it comes close and, more important, makes me sigh happily every time I take a bite.

THE BAZAAR BY JOSÉ ANDRÉS
SLS HOTEL
1701 Collins Ave., Miami Beach: 305-455-2999
www.thebazaar.com
CUISINE: Tapas/Small Plates, Spanish
DRINKS: Full Bar
SERVING: Dinner
The swanky SLS Hotel had to have a big name to headline its "important" restaurant, and it's hard to top **José Andrés**. Fun place with a creative menu serving items like Dragonfruit Ceviche and Caprese Salad. Delicious cocktails. Great selection of Serrano and Ibérico hams, Catalan pork sausage, codfish fritters (a specialty), seared scallops. Though I never liked it, everybody raves about the Dulce de Leche dessert. $$$$

BIG PINK
157 Collins Ave.; 305-532-4700; 305-531-0888 for delivery.
http://www.mylesrestaurantgroup.com/
CUISINE: American, Diner
DRINKS: Full bar
SERVING: Breakfast, lunch and dinner from 8am.
NEIGHBORHOOD: SoFi (South of Fifth)
TVs for sports fans. You'd never know it to walk in this joint, but the same guy who owns **Prime 112** a couple of blocks away owns this place slinging out chicken wings and draft beer for pennies on the dollar compared to the higher-profile place. Really good American diner food. Popular with locals who wouldn't be caught dead at Prime 112. $$

BODEGA TAQUERIA Y TEQUILA
1220 16th St, Miami Beach, 305-704-2145
www.bodegataqueria.com
CUISINE: Mexican

DRINKS: Full Bar
SERVING: Lunch & Dinner
PRICE RANGE: $$
This local's favorite serves over-the-top Mexican street food and features a taco truck inside. Great choice for lunch or late-night munching. The real star of this place is the hidden bar.

BOLIVAR
841 Washington Ave., Miami Beach: 305-305-0801
www.bolivarmiamibeach.com
CUISINE: Peruvian, Colombian, Venezuelan
DRINKS: Full Bar
SERVING: Lunch, Dinner
Classic South American dishes served. Delicious menu items include salmon in Creole sauce with cilantro rice. Romantic atmosphere and excellent service. $$

BYBLOS
1545 Collins Ave, Miami Beach, 786-864-2990
www.byblosmiami.com
CUISINE: Mediterranean / Middle Eastern
DRINKS: Full bar
SERVING: Dinner
PRICE RANGE: $$$
This place offers a great dining experience in a plush atmosphere that makes you imagine what Nikki Beach might look like in Greece. (Or anywhere else out there.) High ceilings, lush booths, pillows, divans, lounges. The cuisine is a mishmash of items from Jordan, Israel, Lebanon. All very tasty and very expertly prepared. This place opened after the Canadian owners had a big success with a Byblos in Toronto. Unlike a lot of other upmarket restaurants flooding into Miami, this one is not pretentious and full of itself. Even if you don't like Lamb Ribs, I urge you to get it as a starter. They marinate them 24 hours

before they get a rubbing of molasses. Then the ribs are plunked into a blend of Eastern spices & crushed nuts and seeds (called dukka) that results in a crunchy texture to the finished product. Anyway, they are really good. There are numerous delicious dishes like Duck Kibbeh, Eggplant Dumplings and Jeweled Rice. If you know someone who knows this kind of food, treat them to dinner here—they'll help you order. Otherwise, trust the very friendly staff. The wine list is more expensive than it ought to be, so order wisely. Or drink beer, as I do, even better.

CARROT EXPRESS
1755 Alton Rd, 305-535-1379
https://eatcarrotexpress.com/
CUISINE: Vegetarian/Juice Bar
DRINKS: No Booze
SERVING: 10 a.m. – 9 p.m.
PRICE RANGE: $$
Counter-service spot offering a menu of vegan & vegetarian fare. Favorites: Chicken melt on pita and Tuna wrap. Great smoothies.

CASA TUA
1700 James Ave.; 305-673-1010
www.casatualife.com/
CUISINE: Italian, with a flair
DRINKS: Full bar
SERVING: Lunch weekdays 12pm – 3pm; dinner nightly from 7
Very hot spot. The best food. Upstairs they have a VERY nice lounge, but it's private now. (I used to love the upstairs lounge for a drink or two before dining below.) But plebeians can still get in for lunch and dinner. But the food doesn't get much better. A lovely starter is the veal tartare with artichokes and truffles. They have a veal tenderloin marinated in lime served with an au gratin of

zucchini that melts in your mouth; also braised veal cheeks that are sublime. They have two risottos that are standouts: the one with the Maine lobster and the one with black truffles. Superior. The lunch menu is very abbreviated. Here, splurge on dinner, even if you might get treated like the ultimate Outsider.

CHALAN ON THE BEACH
1580 Washington Ave.; 305-532-8880
No web site
CUISINE: Peruvian
DRINKS: Beer & wine
SERVING: Lunch and dinner daily
It looks like a trashy dump on the outside, but once you slide indoors, you can expect some of the best Peruvian food to be had in Miami. And cheap, too. No other Latin America culture prepares seafood as well as Peruvians, in my view. If you're not familiar with this cuisine, the menu will dazzle you. $$

CHEESEBURGER BABY
1505 Washington Ave.; 305-531-7300
CUISINE: the great American burger
DRINKS: beer & wine
SERVING: lunch and dinner daily. Delivery day and night
www.cheeseburgerbaby.net
There's been a proliferation of burger joints on South Beach in the last couple of years, but these are without question the **JUICIEST BURGERS** in South Beach. You can't beat this joint anywhere. All beef is certified Angus, the buns baked locally and the hand-cut their own toppings. The place has a great dive atmosphere. The food, however, is anything but. Counter seating. Only female-owned burger joint and food truck in Miami, since 2001. You go, girls!

CHOTTO MATTE
1664 Lenox Ave, Miami Beach, 305-690-0743
https://chotto-matte.com/miami/
CUISINE: Japanese/Peruvian
DRINKS: Full bar
SERVING: Lunch & Dinner
PRICE RANGE: $$$$
NEIGHBORHOOD: Lincoln Road
Upscale hidden gem located off iconic Lincoln Road with a menu of Nikkei (Japanese & Peruvian) cuisine served "tapas" size. (It's an offshoot of a hip trendy place in London.) There's a dramatic cluster of palm trees raised in the center island behind the bar, and this stands below a very tall atrium that gives the room a majestic ambience. As good as the food is, my advice would be to avoid the weekends, when they start the DJ music as early as 8, making conversation completely impossible. Service drags on. I was once there for over 3 hours and hated every minute of it. Better to come any night but Friday or Saturday. Beautiful décor. Spacious bar with a lively scene. Better yet, do it for lunch unless you want the excitement generated by a crowded place. Favorites: Lobster tempura and Wagyu dumplings. Hang out at the bar for one of their creative cocktails. (I know because I went to the bar more than once to get a drink when the waiter kept avoiding our table.)

CLEO SOUTH BEACH
1776 Collins Ave, Miami Beach, 305-534-2536
www.sbe.com/cleosouthbeach
CUISINE: Mediterranean/Middle Eastern
DRINKS: Full Bar
SERVING: Dinner
PRICE RANGE: $$$
Located in the hip Redbury Hotel, this modern eatery offers a nice menu of creative Eastern Mediterranean fare.

The owners came in from L.A. to launch this place and they brought an extremely competent staff to get things rolling. A very welcoming atmosphere. Menu picks include: Grilled octopus and Tuna Tartare. Nice large bar, which is where you'll find me chatting with the bartender, who makes a powerfully effective Manhattan with Makers Mark.

DORAKU
1104 Lincoln Rd.; 305-695-8383
CUISINE: Japanese/Sushi.
DRINKS: Full bar; SERVING: lunch and dinner daily;
www.dorakusushi.com.
Among the dozen places on Lincoln Road where you can get sushi (and I've eaten in all of them multiple times because that's my job), this is the one I always come back to when I'm not forced by work to go elsewhere. (Has one of the few lively bar scenes among Lincoln Road restaurants and a nice if unpublicized Happy Hour good for food as well as drinks.) $$$

DRUNKEN DRAGON
1424 Alton Rd, Miami Beach, 305-397-8556
www.drunkendragon.com
CUISINE: Asian Fusion / Korean
DRINKS: Full Bar
SERVING: Dinner
PRICE RANGE: $$
This exceedingly popular Korean eatery featuring Asian Fusion and BBQ took over an old Cuban market and it's become wildly popular, so much so you'll need to book ahead. South Beach's first Korean barbecue restaurant offers tableside grilling and modern Asian tapas.

ESTIATORIO MILOS BY COSTAS SPILIADIS
730 First St., Miami Beach: 305-604-6800

www.estiatoriomilos.com
CUISINE: Greek, Seafood
DRINKS: Full Bar
SERVING: Lunch, Dinner
The name alone tells you how "important" they are. When did restaurants become movies, with the director's name above the title? "A Steven Spielberg Eatery." But they do deliver the goods here: incredible choice of seafood shipped in from Morocco, Tunisia, Portugal, Nova Scotia and Greece. Though they have a great selection of meats, you'll want to focus on the seafood here. If you want to savor their excellent food but don't want to pay the bill (this is one of the most expensive places in town), stop in for lunch when they have a prix fixe menu for less than $30. I come here for lunch at least once a month, dinner once a year. Excellent wine list, almost all Greek selections that are light and refreshing. $$$$

FOGO DE CHAO
836 First St.; 305-672-0011

https://fogodechao.com/location/miami/
CUISINE: Brazilian Steakhouse
DRINKS: Full bar
SERVING: lunch weekdays; dinner nightly
NEIGHBORHOOD: SoFi (South of Fifth)
Great experience. Massive salad bar comes with your meal (which is *prix fixe*, and it's all you can eat). Waiters carrying swords with grilled meat move table-to-table supplying you with an endless amount of different kinds of meat. If you're from the middle of nowhere, this is a must. They won't have this in your town. (I'm just glad they have it in this town!) Excellent and reasonable wine list and the most attentive staff. (It's a little heavy for lunch, so if you come for lunch, make this your big meal of the day.) $$

FORTE DEI MARMI
150 Ocean Dr, Miami Beach,786-276-3095
www.fdmmiami.com
CUISINE: Italian/Seafood
DRINKS: Full Bar
SERVING: Dinner, Sunday Brunch
PRICE RANGE: $$$
Chic eatery offering a creative menu of Italian classics in a lovely setting. Pink bougainvillea hangs from the arched entrance. Favorites: Linguine Alla Nerano and Calamari Tagliatelle. Great place for Sunday Brunch. If you're having dessert you must try the Sicilian's Pistachio Crème Brulee, an interesting version of crème brulee served with chocolate gelato. All-Italian wine list.

JAYA AT SETAI
2001 Collins Ave., 855-923-7899
CUISINE: Contemporary, Indian
DRINKS: Full bar
SERVING: 7am to midnight daily

www.thesetaihotel.com
Just plain excellent. Fine food beautifully served. In a town with several really good Sunday brunches, this one excels. It's not the cheapest, but it may very well be the best.

JOE'S STONE CRAB $$$
11 Washington Ave.; 305-673-0365
www.joesstonecrab.com
CUISINE: American, Seafood
DRINKS: Full bar
SERVING: lunch, dinner daily October-May; summer hours vary
NEIGHBORHOOD: SoFi (South of Fifth)
The most famous restaurant on South Beach. Opened in 1913, they still serve up great stone crabs. If you don't like stone crabs (I actually met someone who didn't!), order anything on their menu. It's all great. You can even get half a fried chicken for $6.95, some of the best fried chicken you've ever had. If you've never been here before,

this is a must. But it's much easier at lunch than dinner to get in. If you have to go to dinner, go early, around 6, and getting in won't be a problem. Later than that, expect a wait of an hour or two, longer on weekends. (A great place to eat at the bar if you're alone or a couple.) No reservations.

JOE'S TAKEAWAY
11 Washington Ave., 305-673-0365
CUISINE: American
DRINKS: Beer & Wine
SERVING: breakfast, lunch, dinner daily; closed in summer
www.joesstonecrab.com
NEIGHBORHOOD: SoFi (South of Fifth)
They even serve breakfast (I have breakfast here 3 times a week when I am in town), and things here are cheaper than you think. There are dozens of restaurants on South Beach that charge more than Joe's for inferior quality food and service. (Try their fried chicken—you get a half-chicken for an astounding $6.95.) $$

JUVIA
1111 Lincoln Rd., Miami Beach: 305-763-8272
www.juviamiami.com
CUISINE: Asian Fusion, Japanese, Seafood
DRINKS: Full Bar
SERVING: Lunch, Dinner
Gorgeous setting with penthouse views of South Beach. Creative menu with dishes like Unagi with chocolate and Binchotan-grilled tenderloin. Dine early for sunset view. There are surprisingly few places where you can get an overview of South Beach. This is one of them. If you're on a budget, go to the bar, enjoy the view and eat somewhere else. **Shake Shack's** in the same building.) Order a beer, which will cost less than a glass of wine and last longer. $$$$

KATSUYA BY STARCK
SLS Hotel
1701 Collins Ave., Miami Beach: 305-455-2995
www.sbe.com/katsuya/south-beach
CUISINE: Sushi
DRINKS: Full Bar
SERVING: Dinner
A chic two-level sushi restaurant in South Beach's new **SLS Hotel** with a menu of small starters, sushi, robata and other hot dishes. Extensive list of sake and specialty cocktails. $$$$

LA SANDWICHERIE
229 14 St., Miami Beach: 305-532-8934
www.lasandwicherie.com
CUISINE: Sandwiches; French
DRINKS: beer & wine
SERVING: 8 a.m. to 5 a.m. (till 6 a.m. on weekends)
Whoever figured this place would last for 20 years? I first came across this placed stumbling out of South Beach's oldest (and still the best) dive bar across the street, the **Deuce**. It's just a little spot, with an outdoor counter and no indoor seating. Nice sandwiches ($6-$9) always served on crunchy baguettes of soft croissants. You can sort of make each sandwich to order. It's like the archetypal Subway, only they wish.

LT STEAK & SEAFOOD
The Betsy Hotel
1440 Ocean Dr., 305-673-0044
www.thebetsyhotel.com/dining
CUISINE: Steaks-some seafood
DRINKS: Full bar
SERVING: Breakfast, lunch and dinner daily
Chef Laurent Tourondel's entry in the South Beach restaurant sweepstakes. Not just the steaks for which he's famous, but Dover sole and other seafood specialties as well. Breakfast for two can run you a cool $60. A recent dinner for four cost over $500. So... make it a special occasion, because it IS special. Extremely talented and attentive waiters. (The best bacon in the world if you have a chance to breakfast here. Worth a special trip for the bacon and scones in the morning.) This is one of those very rare spots on Ocean Drive that I recommend, an oasis among the desert of Tourist Traps populating this once lovely street now turned into a monster of mediocrity by greedy landlords and a city that could use a heightened sensibility to appreciate what this street cold have become.

LA MODERNA
1874 Bay Rd, Miami Beach, 305-397-8419
www.lamoderna-miami.com
CUISINE: Italian / Pizza
DRINKS: Full bar
SERVING: Lunch & Dinner
PRICE RANGE: $$
Trattoria offering a creative menu of Neapolitan pies and rustic-modern pastas. Menu picks include: Spaghetti with caviar and Oyster and crispy leeks. Great creative craft cocktails.

LOS FUEGOS
Faena Hotel
3201 Collins Ave, Miami Beach, 786-655-5600
www.faena.com
CUISINE: Argentine
DRINKS: Full bar
SERVING: breakfast, lunch & dinner daily
PRICE RANGE: $$$$
NEIGHBORHOOD: Middle Beach
Located in one of the more elegant hotel properties in town, the Faena. There's a striking circular chandelier in the middle of the dining room with a hundred small lights that when working together create a masterful fixture. Then there's a bold sculpture of a unicorn on a pedestal in the other part of the place that, when I first saw it, brought to mind the Golden Calf made by the Israelites when Moses went up to Mount Sinai. Looking around the Faena, the feeling creeps up on you that you're in the midst of over-the-top extravagance for which there is little excuse. (Not to be a party pooper.) There's an outdoor patio area with a bar where you can sit if the weather's good. Worth coming here for a drink just to take in the gorgeous interiors. South American eatery featuring seafood, steak and classic regional dishes of the Argentine. Impressive wine list (with eye-rolling prices to match). Favorites: 30oz bone-in ribeye with chimichurri and Seabass 'en Papillote'.

LUCALI
1930 Bay Rd, Miami Beach, 305-695-4441
www.lucali.com/
CUISINE: Italian
DRINKS: Full bar
SERVING: Dinner plus Lunch on Sat & Sun
PRICE RANGE: $$
NEIGHBORHOOD: Sunset Harbour

Nice little eatery serving brick-oven pizzas and salads. You can smell the wood they use in the oven—it's stacked up right by the bar. Bar offers Italian wines, craft draft and bottled beers. Pizzas are their specialty, but they also offer calzones, wings, meatballs, and desserts. Outdoor seating as well.

LURE FISHBAR
1601 Collins Ave, Miami Beach, 305-695-4550
Loews Hotel
www.lurefishbar.com
CUISINE: Seafood/Sushi
DRINKS: Full bar
SERVING: Dinner
PRICE RANGE: $$$
Located in the Loews Hotel, everything is nautical-themed from the décor to the cocktails. Classic seafood menu offering great surf 'n' turf, sushi, and oysters. Try their tasty signature crafted cocktails (most have at least six ingredients). Save room for their delicious Key Lime Pie made with house-made Graham Cracker and roasted white chocolate.

MACCHIALINA TAVERNA RUSTICA
820 Alton Rd., Miami Beach: 305-534-2124
www.macchialina.com
CUISINE: Italian
DRINKS: Full bar
SERVING: Dinner
This intimate (maybe 50 seats inside, with some on the street outside) eatery serves top-notch Italian fare including great dishes like Eggplant & Mozzarella and Wagyu Carpaccio. While the food is undeniably good, everything on the menu is $10 less at **Oliver's** just around the corner. (Of course, the food at Oliver's is a peg or two or even three down in quality than this gourmet place.)

And the wine list here is not very friendly. I don't remember a single bottle under $50. Not cool. But I still come here often because I love it. (I just don't order wine.) The vibe here is one of the coolest in town. And trust me, it's ALWAYS packed. When I go, I arrive promptly when they open at 6 so I can grab a seat and eat at the bar. Fills up fast. $$$

MATADOR ROOM
Edition Hotel
2901 Collins Ave, Miami Beach, 786-257-4600
www.matadorroom.com
CUISINE: Spanish/Caribbean
DRINKS: Full Bar
SERVING: Dinner, Late Night
PRICE RANGE: $$$
This upscale eatery offers Jean-Georges Vongerichten's take on Latin cuisine, with some dishes copied from the chef's ABC Cocina in New York. Here you can dine on a seasonal menu of small and large plates. Beautiful oval dining room and bar that overlooks the pool. Menu picks include: Grilled Octopus and Short Ribs. Creative cocktails. The best thing about this place is that it's located off the stunning hotel lobby. I hadn't expected all that white marble. The way they up-lighted the potted palm to get the fronds to cast muted shadows on the white ceiling gave the place a very modern take on a noir look from the 1930s or '40s. Superior design concept, I must say. The hotel bar is expensive and boring, to my taste, and the restaurant also is stuffy and shrug-inducing, requiring an effort. On the weekends, the place is packed as party-goers head to the **Basement** nightclub downstairs.

MISTER 01
1680 Michigan Ave, Miami Beach, 305-397-8189
www.mister01.com

CUISINE: Pizza
DRINKS: Beer & Wine
SERVING: Lunch and Dinner
PRICE RANGE: $$
NEIGHBORHOOD: Lincoln Road
A popular pizza spot that takes reservations, believe it or not. Neapolitan-style pies, antipasti and salads. Small bare-bones eatery but the pizza is the best. Try the Nutella pizza for a real treat. Vegetarian options.

MONTY'S SUNSET
300 Alton Rd, Miami Beach, 305-672-1148
www.montyssobe.com
CUISINE: Seafood
DRINKS: Full Bar
SERVING: Lunch & Dinner
PRICE RANGE: $$
NEIGHBORHOOD: South Beach
This is about the only place you can go for lunch and use the pool. It's right on the water facing the Third Street Marina, so you get to see all the boats tied up on the docks. Large outdoor tiki hut bar attracts a big crowd. Popular

waterfront seafood eatery with a raw bar & the usual fish shack fare. Besides the Stone crabs this place features live music, DJs, TVs for sports and happy hour special. Favorites: Lobster bisque, grouper tacos and Fried Shrimp. Another plus is the Free Parking – a rarity on South Beach.

MR. CHOW
W South Beach Hotel
2201 Collins Ave., 305-695-1695
www.mrchow.com
CUISINE: Chinese
DRINKS: Full bar
SERVING: Dinner nightly
The food's very nice, as a rule, but of course it ought to be. Can't go wrong with the Beijing chicken, the famous green prawns, whatever lobster dish they're serving, and my favorite: the crispy beef and duck. (Oh, and get the fried rice.) They've gone all-out on the décor, and worth a trip just to see the place.

MY CEVICHE
235 Washington Ave., Miami Beach: 305-397-8710
www.myceviche.com
CUISINE: Seafood, Peruvian
DRINKS: No Alcohol
SERVING: Lunch, Dinner

It's a little hole-in-the wall but co-owners Roger Duarte and James Beard Award-nominated chef Sam Gorenstein are serving delicious ceviche. Everybody I know who loves ceviche LOVES this place. Very cheap, too. $$

NAIYARA
1854 Bay Rd, Miami Beach, 786-275-6005
www.naiyara.com
CUISINE: Thai/Japanese
DRINKS: Full bar
SERVING: Dinner
PRICE RANGE: $$$
Popular eatery serving up a creative menu of Thai street food, sushi and Asian specialties. Favorites include: Crispy bok choy, Chicken dumplings, and Creamy ramen noodle soup with prawns. Unique cocktails. Reservations recommended.

NAUTILUS CABANA CLUB
Nautilus Hotel
1825 Collins Ave, Miami Beach, 786-483-2650
www.arlohotels.com
CUISINE: Latin American
DRINKS: Full Bar
SERVING: Breakfast, Lunch & Dinner
PRICE RANGE: $$
Beachside eatery with a menu of seafood-focused Mediterranean fare & vegetarian options. Favorites: Steak and fish, Tzatziki and vegetables. Often, they have live music. Great choice for Brunch.

OLIVER'S BISTRO
959 West Ave., Miami Beach: 305-535-3050
CUISINE: American (some Italian)
DRINKS: Full bar
SERVING: breakfast, lunch & dinner daily. (Opens at 9)

www.oliversmiamibeach.com
One of the nicest places frequented by locals. Staff is courteous, the food superior, and their excellent chef hasn't allowed the kitchen to fall off the high standards he set when they first opened. In good weather, you can sit outside and watch the locals stroll by on West Avenue.

Starters: We like the Shrimp & Brie Quesadilla, enhanced with sour cream, black bean relish, salsa and the expected guacamole. Yum. Full range of salads, from Crunchy Chicken to a very nice Cobb; Greek Salad with Grilled Calamari; Spicy Beef Salad. A lovely Rare Seared Sushi Grade Ahi Tuna Niciose Salad is a winner, too.

Main course favorites: quite a few pasta and risotto dishes stand out, from as simple as you can get (Linguini Aglio e Olio or Spaghetti & Meatballs). Steak frites platter is good. One of my favorite things here is to order the mussels with spicy sausage in a tomato garlic broth and have them toss a side of pasta into it: for about $20 you get a great meal, half of which you can take home. (They use Italian sausage in the dish instead of the chorizo you get everywhere else in town, making the dish much, much more flavorful.)

Serves "late breakfast" till 2:30 daily, and has a full brunch menu on weekends. Also has a very nice Vegetable Plate. $$$

PAPI STEAK
736 1st St, Miami Beach, 305-800-PAPI
http://papisteak.com/
CUISINE: Steakhouse
DRINKS: Full Bar
SERVING: Dinner
PRICE RANGE: $$$$
NEIGHBORHOOD: SoFi (South of Fifth)
Intimate dining featuring classic dishes and prime meats. They're offering something a little more subdued and

civilized than the circus you have to endure at nearby Prime 112 (although big shot Latin American blowhards with their hookers can be seen here as well). The interior is quite dramatic, with highly colorful wall treatments over the plush red velvet banquettes. Specialty cocktails and impressive wine list. Most items are big enough to share. (So is the bill, LOL!) Favorites: Papi Steak (a huge ribeye) and Latkes with crème fraiche.

PARRILLA LIBERTY & PIZZA
1255 Washington Ave.; 305-532-7599
CUISINE: Argentine
DRINKS: beer & wine
SERVING: Daily noon – midnight
www.laparrillaliberty.com. A
All the favorites from Argentina but cheap, cheap, cheap! (A little more chewy than great meat, but still… don't eat here if you have dentures.) $

PLANTA
850 Commerce St, Miami Beach, 305-397-8513
www.plantarestaurants.com
CUISINE: Vegetarian
DRINKS: Full bar

SERVING: Breakfast & Brunch, Lunch, Dinner
PRICE RANGE: $$$$
NEIGHBORHOOD: SoFi (South of Fifth)
Just a few feet from Joe's Stone Crab, across from Joe's self-parking lot, is this Vegetarian eatery that's well worth your time. This is most certainly NOT your typical Vegetarian spot, but very high-end, with a creative menu that is equal to the stunning interiors they've got to offer here. Lots of high windows and skylight treatment. I eat veggies every day, but I seldom order vegetarian because the food is usually so uninspired. Not so here. offering an impressive menu featuring flatbreads, croquettes, and steamed dumplings. Try the Buffalo cauliflower pizza. The Crispy Chicken sandwich, for instance, is made with buttermilk fried cauliflower, daikon, carrot, cilantro, challah bun, tajin fries. You won't believe how good it tastes. Reservations recommended.

PRIME ONE TWELVE
112 Ocean Dr. (The Browns Hotel), 305-532-8112
www.mylesrestaurantgroup.com

CUISINE: Steakhouse
DRINKS: Full bar
SERVING: Lunch from 11:30 weekdays, dinner from 6:30. NEIGHBORHOOD: SoFi (South of Fifth)
Basketball players and other celebs come here to see, be seen, and order the 48 oz. Porterhouse. If you want to go here but not "go there," go for lunch at the bar and order a sandwich and a beer. There's an appetizer here, the truffled deviled eggs with caviar for $20 that ought to be tried before you die. (In fact, this dish will HELP you die, but you'll go down smiling!) Oh, just a warning: this will be the MOST EPENSIVE place for lunch or dinner you can go on South Beach. I can't think of anywhere more ridiculously priced. ***Tip:*** Miles, the guy that owns this place, also owns a busy diner popular with locals (like me) right around the corner on Second Street, called **BIG PINK**. Of course, you don't get the big prime steaks, it's diner food, but the quality is great, the portions huge and the prices much less draconian. (Those same famous jocks also go to Big Pink, by the way.)

SARDINIA-ENOTECA RISTORANTE $$$
1801 Purdy Ave, 305-531-2228
CUISINE: Italian-Sardinian
DRINKS: Full bar
SERVING: Daily noon – midnight
www.sardinia-ristorante.com
Look over the menu online. This is Sardinian, *not* Italian. I love the little cheese and meat boards where they let you mix and match cheeses with meats. The side dishes (roasted beets, braised baby Brussels sprouts) are great. My favorite starter is sautéed chicken livers with fava beans. A meal by itself. (The wines are from Sardinia too, but tend to be lighter than the best Italian wines, but they're eminently quaffable.)

SCARPETTA
Fontainebleau
4441 Collins Ave, 305-674-4660 / 305-538-2000
www.fontainebleau.com/web/dining/scarpetta
CUISINE: Italian
DRINKS: Full bar
SERVING: Dinner daily from 5:30.
NEIGHBORHOOD: Middle Beach
There's no question that when this dowager hotel reopened after a renovation that costs tens of millions of dollars (2010), this was the prize jewel of all the well-hyped restaurants. When you arrive at the hotel, they will have to tell you how to get there, it's so far away from where an Uber will drop you. (And I had to stop twice to ask directions.) When you get to the space, you'll find it's just the opposite of what you expected: a small, intimate, charmingly decorated room that feels like it's anywhere but here. The food is nothing short of spectacular. You've never had pasta that was this delicate, unless you've been to Chef Scott Conant's eatery in New York. It's the same great food. Favorite starters are the crispy fritto misto and the creamy polenta. There's also a Japanese mackerel tartar that jumps right out at you. Bypass the steaks, chops and seafood and focus on his pasta dishes as your entrée, especially the scialatelli and the agnolotti dal plin. You'll go nuts. Don't miss the Osso Bucco.

SEGAFREDO ESPRESSO
1040 Lincoln Rd.; 305-673-0047
http://www.sze-originale.com/
CUISINE: Café, Appetizers
DRINKS: Full bar
SERVING: lunch & dinner daily

I don't recommend but 3 or 4 places on all of Lincoln Road, for a good reason—the restaurants here are almost as much of an unmitigated rip-off as the terrible places you find on Ocean Drive. This one, however, is different. The aim here is to reflect the lifestyle of Italy's famously fun and charming coffee bars. It's hard to beat the ambience here – lounging on a sofa out on Lincoln Road with a coffee or a drink or a meal. The food is very reasonably priced and the quality is very exceptional. I know the owner quite well, and when I go to Lincoln Road, I invariably drop in here. There's a tiny bar inside where you can often get a seat if it's packed outside. (That's where you'll find me.) The colorful fountain is by famed Cuban artist Carlos Alves. $$$

SMITH & WOLLENSKY
1 Washington Ave.; 305-673-2800
www.smithandwollensky.com
CUISINE: American, Steakhouse, Seafood
DRINKS: Full bar
SERVING: lunch and dinner daily

NEIGHBORHOOD: SoFi (South of Fifth)
Sorry, but no visit to South Beach is complete without dropping by this place, even if it's for a drink at the outside bar overlooking Gov't Cut where you can see the boat traffic coming into and out of the Port of Miami. They have a cold seafood platter that's killer, and the million-dollar view is free!

SPIGA
1228 Collins Ave, Miami Beach, 305-534-0079
www.spigarestaurant.com
CUISINE: Italian / Seafood
DRINKS: Beer & Wine Only
SERVING: Dinner
PRICE RANGE: $$$
I tend to forget about this intimate eatery offers a menu of Northern Italian cuisine including great seafood and homemade pastas. Why? Because it's tucked inside the lobby of the tiny and elegant Impala Hotel. It's been here for years and I just love it. Outdoor garden dining. Nice wine list.

STILTSVILLE FISH BAR
1787 Purdy Ave, Miami Beach, 786-724-1671
www.stiltsvillefishbar.com
CUISINE: Seafood, Tapas/Small Plates, Cocktail Bars
DRINKS: Full Bar
SERVING: Dinner, Lunch & Dinner Sat - Sun
PRICE RANGE: $$$-$$$$
Casual eatery featuring big open garage style window/doors. It's a lot less hectic and bustling during the week, while on weekends, it's one of "the" places to be. Without a reservation on the weekends, you'll get turned away. As "rustic" as they've tried to make this place, there's nothing rustic about the food. It's smart, sophisticated, expertly prepared—everything. Creative

menu offering fresh options from fish to vegetables. The fish is delivered daily from fishermen working in Key Largo, Key West and here in Miami. Very fish-centric menu. The leftover fish parts are smoked to make a very nice dip which you ought to get as a starter for the whole table to sample. A popular dish is the whole fried snapper. (Don't worry about forgetting this—the waiters push it, actually.) It's visually striking when it lands on your table. Impressive salads. Favorites: Shrimp 'N Grits and Lobster Mac N' Mushrooms. The chef is noted for his fried chicken (which he debuted at **Yardbird** over near Lincoln Road). But don't get it—it's far too expensive. (Instead, get the fried chicken next time you're at **Joe's Stone Crab**—you'll get a half chicken for what it costs for a single piece here.) Dining room includes bar (with perhaps the most uncomfortable bar stools in all Christendom) and lounge area.

STUBBORN SEED
101 Washington Ave, Miami Beach, 786-322-5211
www.stubbornseed.com
101 Washington Ave., Miami Beach
CUISINE: American (New)/Seafood
DRINKS: Full Bar
SERVING: Dinner; closed Mondays
PRICE RANGE: $$$-$$$$
NEIGHBORHOOD: SoFi (South of Fifth)
Opened by Top Chef 13 winner Jeremy Ford. This very small eatery offers a menu of seasonal American cuisine created by a master at his craft. Tip: Try the Chef's Tasting Menu which has some of the menu's best. Favorites: Smoked foie gras, Maine Lobster poached in butter, lavash (chicken liver butter), warm celery root, and the Slow Cooked Florida Snapper. Craft cocktails. I hope to God this place stays open more than a year. I almost skipped putting this place in my book because so many of

this “type” of place never make it. The food is so good I am praying. Yes, the portions are small and the prices are steep, but still… this place is a superior achievement. I don’t think the name helps, but as long as he keeps cooking the way he’s cooking, I don’t give a damn what he calls it.

SUGAR FACTORY
1060 Ocean Dr, Miami Beach, 305-535-9773
www.sugarfactory.com/miami
CUISINE: American (New) / Desserts
DRINKS: Full bar
SERVING: Breakfast, Lunch & Dinner
PRICE RANGE: $$
Located in the beautiful art deco Hotel Victor, this newly-redecorated 3,000 square foot brasserie offers a candy shop up front and patio dining overlooking Ocean Drive and the ocean. Known for their world-famous Couture Pops, creative cocktails, the menu also offers pancakes, crepes, salads, burgers, and creative desserts.

Thomas Keller hard at work

SURF CLUB RESTAURANT
9011 Collins Ave., Surfside, 305-768-9440
www.surfclubrestaurant.com
CUISINE: American (Traditional)/Modern European
DRINKS: Full bar
SERVING: Dinner
PRICE RANGE: $$$$
NEIGHBORHOOD: North Beach / Bal Harbour
World-class dining specializing in meats. This is Thomas Keller's spot in what used to be the old private Surf Club, a bastion of "society" since the 1930s. Winston Churchill set up his easel and painted some watercolors here. This place was built in the old club house, and across the high-ceilinged hallway is another restaurant, which I like better than this Keller spot. If you're coming to dinner here, arrive early and have a drink in the spacious bar across the hallway—the architectural details in this space (in the Spanish-Moorish, Mediterranean Revival Robber Baron Style of Addison Mizner) are well worth seeing. Favorites: Rib eye with Foie Gras; the short ribs (braised 48-hours); and Hokkaido scallops. Roasted chicken is prepared and served table-side. (It's flavorful & juicy.) The famous Beef Wellington is so rich you might want to throw up after eating it, though it's a work of art if you can handle it. Delicious desserts.

SUSHI BY BOU
Versace Villa
1116 Ocean Dr, Miami Beach, 305-922-9195
www.sushibybou.com
CUISINE: Japanese/Sushi
DRINKS: Full bar
SERVING: Dinner
PRICE RANGE: $$$$
NEIGHBORHOOD: Ocean Drive

You'll walk up the front steps where the designer Versace was gunned down as he tried to enter his villa back in 1997. On the top floor of the mansion is this intimate counter with only a half dozen seats. Private chef serves. Fresh sushi and creative cocktails. Amazing experience if you want to impress someone. Price includes 17 piece omakase meal. Take a stroll around the interior of Versace's mansion while you're here. I went to quite a few parties in this place when Versace was alive, and it still retains some of the magical excesses of those days (except the people are not as sexy and attractive as they were then). Still quite a sight.

SWEET LIBERTY DRINKS & SUPPLY COMPANY
237-B 20th St, Miami Beach, 305-763-8217
www.mysweetliberty.com
CUISINE: American (New)
DRINKS: Beer & Wine Only
SERVING: Dinner, Brunch on Sundays
PRICE RANGE: $$
NEIGHBORHOOD: Convention Center
Near the Bass Museum and the renovated Convention Center is this hideaway known and frequented by every serious bartender in Miami because it (well, original boss, here, Lermayer) gets credit for spawning the "craft cocktail" trend in Miami. The bartenders here *really* know their shit. It's very unassuming, even down market, but they have cheap oysters during happy hour, and VERY reasonable prices for food. (Cocktails are not outrageously priced.) Favorites: Lobster rolls, fried chicken and Cauliflower nachos. Happy hour specials. A pool table for those interested. Lermayer once said, "The cocktail is America's first epicurean contribution to the world." And unlike all those other places where they serve "craft cocktails," here you'll find no velvet rope and (for Miami) a refreshing absence of bullshit and attitude.

TANUKI
1080 Alton Rd, Miami Beach, 305-615-1055
www.tanukimiami.com
CUISINE: Asian Fusion, Dim Sum, Japanese
DRINKS: Full Bar
SERVING: Dinner only on Monday & Tues, Lunch & Dinner Wed - Sun
PRICE RANGE: $$$
Upscale eatery specializing in sushi, dim sum and wok with some of the finest Japanese, Thai, Korean, Malaysian and Chinese dishes. Favorites: Dim sum and Shanghainese soup dumplings. For a special occasion try their Peking Duck. Great desserts.

TIME OUT MARKET
1601 Drexel Ave, Miami Beach, 786-753-5388
www.timeoutmarket.com
CUISINE: Food Hall
DRINKS: Full bar
SERVING: Lunch & Dinner
PRICE RANGE: $$-$$$
NEIGHBORHOOD: Lincoln Road
Upscale food hall (the original is in Lisbon) with 18 eateries under one roof – everything from Vegan, Pho, Cuban, Mexican, Italian to Cuban ice cream. Two celebrity chefs, Norman Van Aken and Jeremy Ford, also have booths. Bar is in the center, shared by everyone. Prices are a little high and a lot of locals don't come here for that reason, but the place is fun. Big screen TV, Live DJ on weekends. Indoor/outdoor seating.

UNDER THE MANGO TREE
737 Fifth St, 786-558-5103
www.mangotreemiami.com
CUISINE: Juice Bars/Smoothies/Acai Bowls

DRINKS: No Booze
SERVING: 8 a.m. – 6 p.m.
PRICE RANGE: $$
Small counter-serve juice bar with a selection of veggie snacks and sandwiches. Favorites: Marley Acai Bowl and Spicy Kale Melt. Impressive juice selection. Eco-friendly gift items.

VIA EMILIA 9
1120 15th St, Miami Beach,786-216-7150
www.viaemilia9.com
CUISINE: Italian
DRINKS: Beer & Wine Only
SERVING: Lunch & Dinner
PRICE RANGE: $$
NEIGHBORHOOD: near Lincoln Road
This is one of those little "finds" you read guidebooks like this to discover. You'd never stumble onto it by yourself. Just a half-block east of Alton Road is this Italian eatery with a menu of authentic Italian classics and house made Perezpasta. You'll see the Chef Wendy Cacciatori behind the counter cooking almost every night. The place is split into 2 rooms, a diner-counter on one side (behind which he cooks) and am intimate, charming romantic room on the other side of the wall where candlelight flickers on the little tables. (I prefer to sit in the brighter diner side just because I love to watch this guy cook.) His concept was simple when he came to South Beach—he'd only cook dishes you could get on the via Emilia in Italy that happens to run through towns like Bologna, Parma and Modena. If you can't get to Italy anytime soon, you're in luck. Come here. Favorites: Eggplant parmigiana and gnocchi. Well, any of the pastas. They're all great. Nice wine list. Reservations recommended on weekends, when it fills with locals.

VILLA AZUR RESTAURANT & LOUNGE
309 - 23rd St., Miami Beach: 305-763-8688
www.villaazurmiami.com
CUISINE: Italian, Mediterranean
DRINKS: Full Bar
SERVING: Dinner
Went here on my birthday last year. And immediately returned again and again. A bit of French Riviera elegance in South Beach serving delicious dishes like seared tuna with avocado and baby spinach. Actress Halle Berry's boyfriend is one of the owners. A favorite of celebrities and fashionistas. $$$$

MIDDLE & NORTH BEACHES

(from 30th Street in Miami Beach up through Bal Harbour, Surfside, Aventura)

& MIAMI NORTH

This section includes everything in the County north from (and including) the 79th Street Causeway (on the beach side), the northern part of Miami Beach, the few restaurants on the Causeway; Bal Harbour and Bay Harbor. On the mainland, it includes Miami Shores north to the town of North Miami and the inaccurately named City of North Miami Beach (it has no beach and is a hideous, relentlessly tacky part of this town) up to Aventura, where you'll find a few nice places.

CAFÉ AVANTI
732 – 41st St., Miami Beach: 305-538-4400
CUISINE: Italian
DRINKS: full bar
SERVING: L weekdays; D nightly.

www.cafeavanti.com
Frequented by locals who love the food. It's the perfect cozy spot that makes traditional dishes even better than any Italian Grandma. I go there specifically for the linguini con Vongole (they use 2 dozen tender clams in this dish). They also carry the Delaplaine fine sparkling wine from Napa. Save room for the dessert cart. **Jessica**, the owner's daughter, is the hostess with the mostess. There's plenty of parking on the street and a "private" back door entrance. $$$

CARPACCIO
Bal Harbour Shops, 9700 Collins Ave., Bal Harbour: 305-867-7777
www.carpaccioatbalharbour.com
CUISINE: Italian; DRINKS: full bar; SERVING: lunch, dinner
I get up here about 3 or 4 times a year. I sit at the bar because at the tables you're surrounded by the "ladies who lunch" crowd who come up here to shop. The hustle and bustle of the place is fun because you feel like you're in New York. (Often, waiters forget to tell you the specials. Ask for them. I almost never order off the menu any more. The specials are always that good.) $$$

HAKKASAN
Fontainebleau, 4441 Collins Ave., Miami Beach: 786-276-1388
www.hakkasan.com
CUISINE: Chinese
DRINKS: full bar
SERVING: nightly from 6; *dim sum* lunch weekends, 12-3.
I must say that Chinese food has always been Chinese food to me. By that, I mean the concept of "gourmet" Chinese food has similarly seemed to me like a misnomer.

But years ago I went to a place in London and then a place down in Miami called Christine Lee's, and my opinion changed instantly. When it's done right, there is no better food than Chinese, and Hakkasan proves the point. Anything you select from the extensive menu will please. But I'm partial to the crisp-skinned roasted duck. I have to have it every trip. $$$$

LA CÔTE

Fontainebleau, 4441 Collins Ave., Miami Beach: 305-674-4710
www.fontainebleau.com
CUISINE: American; some European
DRINKS: full bar
SERVING: lunch, early dinner (till 7 p.m.)
www.fontainebleau.com
Flatbreads, salads, sandwiches. Second floor of the pool deck at this famous hotel. A great place to look over the ocean. Believe it or not, most of the places you can eat in the hotels lining the water don't have water views, obstructed as they are by sand dunes, sea oats, berms, and other manmade obstacles. But here, you're above it all.

LE ZOO

BAL HARBOUR SHOPS
9700 Collins Ave, 305-602-9663
www.lezoo.com
CUISINE: French
DRINKS: Beer & Wine Only
SERVING: Lunch & Dinner
PRICE RANGE: $$$
NEIGHBORHOOD: Bal Harbour
Popular brasserie with an authentic French feel. It's like sitting on the sidewalk at a Parisian café. Except you're surrounded by the upscale shops like Prada, Chanel and Saks. It's right next door to the old standby that's been in

Bal Harbour for decades, Carpaccio. But I always choose this place over Carpaccio. It's located right at the valet, so you're in for a treat if you like to look at expensive cars. Aston Martins, Bugattis, Lamborghinis, Rolls Royces, you name it. There's a small indoor section, but it's more fun to sit outside. Menu of French classics. Favorites: Veal Piccata and Steak Tartare Du Parc. Though I've had everything on the menu, I gravitate toward the steak frites more often than not. The shoestring fries are expertly cooked. (If they have cucumber soup the day you visit, for God's sake get it. So refreshing and flavorful. I could drink this stuff by the gallon.) Great cocktails and an impressive wine list.

NOBU
4525 Collins Ave., 305-695-3232
www.noburestaurants.com
CUISINE: Japanese
DRINKS: Full bar
SERVING: dinner nightly
South Beach branch of Chef Nobu Matsuhisa's Japanese empire. Among the cold dishes (these are all appetizers), love the yellowtail sashimi with tiny slices of Jalapeno (hot!); salmon kelp roll; sea urchin tiradito; yellowfin tuna tataki; and the monkfish pate with caviar. Standouts among hot starters include their famous rock shrimp tempura; Alaskan king crab tempura; Tasmanian ocean trout with crispy baby spinach. Wide range of Kushiyaki and Tobanyaki specialties as well as the usual sushi and sashimi selections a la carte.

THE PALM
9650 E. Bay Harbor Dr., Bay Harbor Islands: 305-868-7256
CUISINE: steakhouse
DRINKS: full bar
SERVING: dinner from 5
www.thepalm.com
Yes, this is the same Palm as the one in New York. Same menu. Same everything. Still the best steaks anywhere, and all those super side dishes everybody else has copied. Bay Harbor is reached by going north on Collins Avenue. Take a left at 96th Street and go west over the bridge into the little island town of Bay Harbor. Take the first right. It's there on the left. I remember this place when it was called the Post & Paddock. A great room. Worth a trip.
$$$$

SAND BAR + KITCHEN
6752 Collins Ave., Miami Beach, 305-397-8375
https://sandbarkitchen.com/
CUISINE: American / premium quality
DRINKS: full bar; big selection of craft beers
SERVING: lunch and dinner
PRICE RANGE: $$
NEIGHBORHOOD: North Beach
Though it may look like a sports bar, with a couple of dozen monitors hanging on the walls, there's a LOT more to this place than meets the eye. And that secret is in the kitchen, where owner Timmy Wilcox and his team churn out some of the best food served in Miami, from the tuna tartare to the smoked ribs (he has baby backs, St. Louis style, and also great brisket) and chicken that he smokes himself every day or so in a little smoker out on the back patio. The pulled pork sandwich is superior, as is all the food. Mexican street corn, Sandbar Nachos (Refried beans, pico de gallo, cheddar sauce, guacamole, sour cream; add chili, grilled chicken or shrimp), great chicken wings with choice of 6 sauces. Bigger plates like steaks and lamb chops also of the highest quality. He recently added an excellent New Orleans style gumbo to the menu. Drink

specials during games, happy hour, pool table, darts. Well worth a stop.

Pork belly fried buns at Sand Bar + Kitchen

DESIGN DISTRICT
MIDTOWN
WYNWOOD
BISCAYNE CORRIDOR

This section includes the hot new restaurant area "**Midtown**," which is separated from the **Design District** by 36th Street. To the north of 36th Street is the Design District; to the south, Midtown.

Wynwood is just to the south of Midtown.

The **Biscayne Corridor** runs from Downtown up along a seedy but slowly improving Biscayne Boulevard until you hit the Miami Shores area, where things die down.

You'll find a lot of cheap restaurants ($ and $$) here because it's not about tourists, it's about locals.

1-800 LUCKY
143 NW 23rd St, Miami, 305-768-9826
https://www.1800lucky.com/
CUISINE: Asian Fusion
DRINKS: Full bar
SERVING: Lunch
NEIGHBORHOOD: Wynwood
PRICE RANGE: $$-$$$
Food court with an "Industrial look" offering several eateries serving food focused on Asian cuisine – everything from ramen to sushi. Communal tables. Ice cream served outside. Live DJ nights/weekends, when it gets really crowded. Indoor/Outdoor seating. Free Wi-Fi. Pet-friendly.

BEAKER & GRAY
2637 N. Miami Ave, Miami 305-699-2637
www.beakerandgray.com
CUISINE: Modern American/Tapas
DRINKS: Full bar
SERVING: Lunch/Dinner; Dinner only on Sat & Sun
PRICE RANGE: $$
NEIGHBORHOOD: **Wynwood**
This is a cool hot spot near my warehouse (where we keep our wine) and studio (where I write my books). Everybody loves it. The guys here have joined forces to create this innovative eatery offering internationally inspired American fare. While you might have heard of the items on the menu, the way they add their own little twists make everything very distinctive and unique, from the Cuban croquettas to the Chicken fingers, Pumpkin gnocchi and cauliflower. Indoor and outdoor seating.
.

BLUE COLLAR
6730 Biscayne Blvd., Miami: 305-756-0366 / **Biscayne Corridor**
www.bluecollarmiami.com
CUISINE: American
DRINKS: Beer & Wine
SERVING: Lunch, Dinner, Brunch
One of my favorite places in Miami. Chef Danny Serfer and his talented team, working out of a rundown motel on Biscayne, have created one of the "go-to" places in Miami, frequented by highbrow and lowbrow alike. They dish up American comfort food in a small comfortable setting. Pork & Beans, Shrimp & Grits, Braised Brisket, Chicken Cordon Bleu, all worth ordering. One of the things I like about this place is the blackboard listing about 20 vegetable dishes prepared creatively: you can choose 4 of them for $19. Curried cauliflower, grilled asparagus with a blue cheese vinaigrette, warm potato salad with bacon. You get the idea. A meal by itself. Plan on sharing. Delicious desserts. $$

.

ENRIQUETA'S SANDWICH SHOP
186 NE 29th St, Miami: 305-573-4681 /
http://enriquetas.com
CUISINE: Cuban
DRINKS: Beer/Wine
SERVING: Breakfast/Lunch till 3pm.
Really basic Cuban food. Fast, cheap and in the most interesting little spot. (I even put this place in my novel, *The Meter Maid Murders*—it's the place where the robbers stop to get a Cuban sandwich and café con leche.) Breakfast: two eggs, bacon or ham, Cuban toast, café con leche, and a cup of fresh squeezed orange juice, is less than McDonald's. Lunch is just as good and just as reasonable. Everybody in Miami has been here at one time or another. Power players from downtown, cops off the street, construction workers, the UPS driver. It's all locals, no tourists. Although Cubans aren't noted for their punctuality, this place closes promptly at 3, but if you get in by 3, you can order and they won't throw you out.

JIMMY'S EASTSIDE DINER
7201 Biscayne Blvd., Miami: 305-754-3692 / **Biscayne Corridor**
No web site
CUISINE: American/Diner
DRINKS: No Bar
SERVING: Breakfast/ Lunch
Although Jimmy's is your typical greasy spoon diner, the food is always really good. This diner has been around for a very long time, a favorite of locals. When they have it on the menu, try the lamb shank. Delicious. $

JOEY'S ITALIAN CAFÉ
2506 NW 2nd Ave, Miami: 305-438-0488 / **Wynwood**
www.joeyswynwood.com
CUISINE: Italian
DRINKS: Full Bar
SERVING: Lunch / Dinner
Always a lively crowd in this spot owned by Tony Goldman's son, Joey. Updated modern Italian cuisine. Consistently good. $$-$$$

KYU
251 NW 25th St, Miami, 786-577-0150
www.kyumiami.com
CUISINE: Asian Fusion
DRINKS: Full bar
SERVING: Lunch & Dinner; closed Mon
PRICE RANGE: $$
NEIGHBORHOOD: **Wynwood**
Modern hipster eatery with a great menu of Asian fare and creative cocktails. Favorites include: Butter Fried Chicken and Crispy Pork "Guy" (fried pork belly pieces – delicious). Great happy hour menu. Reservations recommended.

MIGNONETTE
210 NE 18th St (corner of 2nd Ave), Miami, 305-374-4635 / **Edgewwater**
www.mignonettemiami.com
CUISINE: American; oyster bar; seafood
DRINKS: Beer & Wine
SERVING: Lunch-Dinner-Brunch
NEIGHBORHOOD: Edgewater (just south of **Wynwood**)
Danny Serfer is famous in these parts for a restaurant further up Biscayne Boulevard, **Blue Collar**, where American comfort food has never been rendered more comfortably. Here, just 2 blocks off Biscayne, and right across the Causeway from South Beach, he has an oyster bar that also serves a wide variety of fresh seafood (from whole hog snapper to scallop crudo). When I go, I sit at the bar and choose from 10 or more oyster selections while drinking a nice Alsatian pinot blanc. (He's only a few blocks from my office.) I usually avoid things like fried clams on Miami menus. But when I tried them here, I realized he was making these dishes the way they would on Cape Cod. Better, even. Try the fried conch as well. By the way, across the street is one of the oldest cemeteries in Miami, well worth a stroll through after stuffing yourself here.

MANDOLIN AEGEAN BISTRO
4312 NE 2nd Ave., Miami: 305-749-9140/ **Design District**
mandolinmiami.com
CUISINE: Greek, with some mixed Mediterranean
DRINKS: Beer/Wine
SERVING: Dinner
Intimate and cozy (and we mean intimate—it's in a small house) with great service and great food. Everybody raves about the white sangria, but it's not for me. (Wine for me.)

I've tried almost every dish on the menu, and there's not a loser in the lot. Outdoors is nice in good weather. $-$$

MC KITCHEN
4141 NE 2nd Ave., Miami, 305-456-9948
www.mckitchenmiami.com
CUISINE: Italian
DRINKS: Full Bar
SERVING: Lunch-Dinner
PRICE RANGE: $$$
NEIGHBORHOOD: Design District
Another fine dining experience in the Design District, just a couple of blocks from pioneering Michael Schwartz's **Michael's Genuine**. Here it's Dena Marino, serving up some of the most prized Italian cuisine in Miami. Spinach lasagna, lovely burrata stuffed with roasted squash, charred octopus drenched in olive oil, spaghetti with shrimp—all are excellent. At lunch one day I had a bloody Mary that the waiter told me had ketchup in it. It sounded so terrible. But after tasting it, I ordered 2 more in rapid succession. (Service can be glacial, so tell them if you want things speeded up.)

MICHAEL'S GENUINE FOOD & DRINK
130 NE 40th St., Miami: 305- 573-5550 / **Design District**
www.michaelsgenuine.com
CUISINE: American
DRINKS: Full bar
SERVING: Lunch / Dinner

Simple décor, but you didn't come to this world-renowned eatery for the décor. **Chef Michael Schwartz** (who rose to some prominence on South Beach at the now closed Nemo's) became an international culinary star when he jumped over to the still-dormant Design District and opened this place focusing on locally sourced ingredients. Menu changes as he sees fit (and I'm glad he saw fit to change it recently, because it had been a while), but you can't go wrong with anything you get here. I even get the chicken here. Plain, simple chicken, which I rarely eat in restaurants because it's usually so incredibly awful. Here, though, it's moist and juicy. Indoor-outdoor. Hard to get in during peak times, even in summer! I always sneak in early, where I usually eat at the bar helping myself liberally from the bowls of radishes they offer). Great staff. Well-balanced wine list, if a bit heavy on the obscure German selections. $$$

MORGANS
28 NE 29th St., Miami: 305-573-9678 / **Wynwood**
themorgansrestaurant.com
CUISINE: American
DRINKS: Full bar
SERVING: B'fast / Lunch / Dinner
They took an old Miami house built in the '30s and turned it into a restaurant. Food's always innovative and trendy. Weekend brunch.

NI.DO. CAFFÈ
7295 Biscayne Blvd., Miami: 305-960-7022 / **Biscayne Corridor**
http://www.nidocaffe.us **WEBSITE DOWN AT PRESSTIME**
CUISINE: Italian
DRINKS: Beer/ Wine
SERVING: Lunch / Dinner

Mozzarella bar. They make it here. Artichoke soufflé, tuna tartare. Very comfy feeling here.

SALUMERIA104
3451 NE First Ave, Miami, 305-424-9588 / **Midtown**
www.salumeria104.com
CUISINE: Italian
DRINKS: Beer & Wine Only
SERVING: Brunch, Lunch & Dinner
PRICE RANGE: $$
Great place for an authentic Italian meal. Menu features a variety of Italian cured meats, pastas, and specials. Menu picks include: Beef lasagna and Antipasto. Nice approachable wine list.

SHOKUDO BY WORLD RESOURCE CAFE
4740 NE 2nd Ave., Miami: 305-758-7782 / **Design District**
www.shokudomiami.com
CUISINE: Asian Fusion
DRINKS: Beer & Wine
SERVING: Lunch, Dinner
Elegant but casual setting serving tasty dishes like Ahi Tuna Poke, SISIG - Sizzling Pork Cheek Buns and house-made dumplings. Impeccable service. $$

ST. ROCH MARKET
140 NE 39th St Suite #241, Miami, 305-722-7100
https://miami.strochmarket.com/ **WEBSITE DOWN AT PRESSTIME**
CUISINE: American (New)
DRINKS: Full bar
SERVING: Breakfast, Lunch, and Dinner
NEIGHBORHOOD: Design District
PRICE RANGE: $$-$$$
This gourmet food hall has an impressive selection of global fare. The design treatment behind the bar, with these scoops cut out of the framework, makes this place look like one of those bars in "Star Wars." But the atmosphere is quite different—all modern, sharp edges, comfortable and welcoming. You could eat lunch and dinner here every day for a week and not scratch the surface. And it would all be great fun. In the middle of the high-end shopping the Design District is known for. Some food halls offer a specialized focus: Italian at **Casa Tua Cicina**, Asian at **1-800-Lucky**, for example. Here you have a wide selection, and it's a great place to try samples of different cuisines. Southern food. Mexican food. Vegan. Italian, Tacos, Ceviche, Sushi, Peruvian, Israeli, Juices, Caribbean, Vietnamese, Asian. Craft cocktail bar. Outdoor seating. Pet friendly.

SUGARCANE RAW BAR GRILL
3252 NE 1st Ave., Miami: 786 369-0353 / **Midtown**
http://www.sugarcanerawbargrill.com
CUISINE: International
DRINKS: Full Bar
SERVING: Lunch/ Dinner
One of the hippest spots in Midtown. All kinds of things going on with this menu, which ranges all over the world. Great raw bar items. I find it very expensive. As if by offering "small plates," they can charge you a lot of money

for a small portion. Still, the food is incredibly good with creative twists and an unusual use of exotic ingredients that will keep your head spinning. How about bacon-wrapped dates? Sounds awful, right? It's not. A big fat date is stuffed with Manchego cheese, linguiça sausage and then wrapped in bacon. Way busy on weekends. Indoor-outdoor. $$$$

WYNWOOD KITCHEN & BAR
2550 NW 2nd Ave., Miami: 305-772-8959 / **Wynwood**
www.wynwoodkitchenandbar.com
CUISINE: American
DRINKS: Beer/ Wine
SERVING: Lunch/ Dinner
Tony Goldman was one of the original New York developers who came to South Beach and saw in the Art Deco District what none of the local developers saw: a gold mine. (When he died in 2012, he still owned the **Park Central Hotel**, his flagship property on **Ocean Drive**.) He never rested on his laurels. He was a big mover and shaker in Wynwood, owning lots of property. What **Craig Robins** wrought in the Design District, Tony Goldman has wrought in Wynwood, to wit: put it on the map. This was his restaurant, and you'll love it. (Son **Joey** owns the eponymous Italian eatery a few feet away.) The way they've decorated the walls with graffiti-style art will remind you why you're not a decorator: who would have thought of this? Food? Very much a bistro style menu, but with influences all over the place. I like the "clay pots," whole meals served in little pots. Choose from chicken curry, the snapper and mussel curry or the braised beef (my favorite of the three: short ribs, sweet soy, caramelized leeks, pickled chilies). Also a standout: the cod fish oreganata and the hanger steak frites. Satisfying sandwiches and salads as well. Don't forget to walk

around the grounds outside to have a look at the graffiti art. $$$

DOWNTOWN-BRICKELL

There really is a lot going on Downtown. From the to the wizardry of Daniel Boulud at **Boulud Sud**, you'll find everything from high quality Indonesian food for $5 at **Bali Café** (no credit cards, cash only) to slices of sashimi at **Zuma** that will cost you twice that for one slice. But it takes some getting used to navigating your way around Downtown. It's congested, everything jammed together, annoying one-way streets, aggravating—and all very exciting. Best is to take someone who knows the area if you're rushed for time.

AREA 31
270 Biscayne Boulevard Way, Miami: 305-424-5234
www.area31restaurant.com
CUISINE: Seafood, Mediterranean
DRINKS: Full Bar
SERVING: B'fast / Lunch / Dinner
Hard to beat the environment they've created down here. From the vantage point of the 16th floor here at the Epic, you get a spectacular view of all the buildings downtown (from inside or outside on their terrace). You feel like you're in a huge metropolis, surrounded by all these glamorous towers. This is NOT the Miami that you get down on street level.

Anyway, the food and drinks are just as spectacular as the view. (Bring your expense account privileges.) The "Area 31" in the name refers to what I presume some official body has determined is a sustainable fishing area that extends from the Carolinas down along the Florida coast, though this can't possibly be true. Still, it's a great marketing hook and you feel free to order anything you want.

Specialties are seafood prepared with a Mediterranean twist.

Lunch: try the pork belly sliders or the smoked turkey club.

Dinner: focus on the fish: yellowtail snapper, the shrimp ravioli are excellent.

What the chef does quite well is use unusual ingredients in all his dishes. His croquettas have tomato jam, diced plantains and cilantro along with the chorizo. His yellowfin tuna will come with radishes, pickled cucumber, quinoa and shoyu.

Here, you're in the hands of a master.

(One of those hands will be in your wallet!) $$$$

BALI CAFÉ
109 NE 2nd Ave., Miami: 305-358-5751
http://balicafe.food93.com/
CUISINE: Indonesia; sushi; Asian fusion
DRINKS: Beer/Wine
SERVING: Lunch / Dinner – **CASH ONLY**
This place is noted because it was written up in the Herald that low-wage Indonesian cruise ship workers who get like half a day off when their ships come in to pick up new passengers head out in droves to this tiny place in Downtown.

Well, everybody else started coming here too. And since the underpaid cruise ship workers are only here once a week, you get the rest of the week to try it out. If you've never had this kind of food, get the *rijsttafel*, which is a kind of sampler. All good food. Cheap. $. CASH ONLY.

THE BAR AT LEVEL 25 (CONRAD HOTEL)
1395 Brickell Ave., Miami: 305-503-6561
www.conradmiami.com

CUISINE: Tapas
DRINKS: Full Bar
SERVING: Lunch / Dinner
They serve sandwiches at lunch and have a raw bar with creative tapas dishes in the evening. Another great view of Downtown. $$$$

BOULUD SUD MIAMI
JW Marriott Marquis, 255 Biscayne Blvd. Way, Miami: 305-421-8800
https://www.bouludsud.com/miami/
CUISINE: French, American
DRINKS: Full Bar
SERVING: Lunch / Dinner
Daniel Boulud's take on American food using Florida ingredients, with his French twist, of course. The result: spectacular. All in the stunning modern setting of this downtown hotel. Very luxe. His burger has gotten famous: a stack that includes *foie gras*, short ribs and black truffles. (Oh, and there's a burger stuffed in there too.) Bring a Lipitor. (Honestly, avoid the burger and focus on the fish.) $$$$

CAPITAL GRILLE
444 Brickell Ave., Miami: 305 374-4500

http://www.thecapitalgrille.com
CUISINE: Steakhouse
DRINKS: Full Bar
SERVING: Lunch weekdays/Dinner nightly
Dry-aged steaks and an award-winning wine list are the draw at this "power lunch" spot. Same sort of menu you already know about. Still, the lobster mac & cheese is a standout. $$$$

CASA TUA CUCINA
Brickell City Centre
70 SW 7th St, Miami, 305-755-0320
https://www.brickellcitycentre.com/
CUISINE: Italian/Mediterranean
DRINKS: Full bar
SERVING: Breakfast, Lunch, and Dinner
NEIGHBORHOOD: Downtown
PRICE RANGE: $$-$$$
Upscale food hall featuring a huge variety of Italian fare – everything from pasta, pizza, salads, and pastries. The space was carved out of the Saks Fifth Avenue store. Each of less than a dozen stalls features a different Italian specialty. You order from a stall, grab a table and a waiter will bring your order, finding you by your number. A wine bar serves all the stalls. Food is really good. Vegan options. Brunch menu in the mornings. Coffee and crafted cocktails. Free Wi-Fi.

CIPRIANI
465 Brickell Ave., Miami, 786-329-4090
www.cipriani.com
CUISINE: Italian
DRINKS: Full Bar
SERVING: Lunch-Dinner daily
PRICE RANGE: $$$$
NEIGHBORHOOD: Brickell

The Cipriani family has made good use of its legendary history, parlaying it into a chain of upmarket restaurants around the world. But they've come a long way since Ernest Hemingway drank in the modest Harry's Bar in Venice. A long way indeed. Ignazio Cipriani is great grandson to Giuseppe, who opened Harry's in 1931. There are 2 levels to this location, and they seat a whopping 400, so it's a massive undertaking. Floor-to-ceiling windows look out onto panoramic views of the Bay. White leather seats and walnut paneling add to the look. The service is professional, but the two times I've been, the waiters were bossy to the point of rudeness. There's way too much steering you to this dish or that wine. Italian specialties are good, but plan on a LONG lunch or dinner. They're in no rush and you better not be.

CRAZY ABOUT YOU
1155 Brickell Bay Dr. #101, Miami: 305-377-4442
www.crazyaboutyourestaurant.com
CUISINE: Mediterranean, Italian, Spanish
DRINKS: Full Bar
SERVING: Lunch / Dinner
Great views. Widely varied menu: chihuahua cheese appetizer; lentil soup, spinach salad; half roasted chicken; red pepper hummus; slow braised steak with creamy arborio rice.

CRUST
668 NW 5TH St., Miami, 305-371-7065
www.**crust**-usa.com
CUISINE: Pizza / Mediterranean
DRINKS: Beer & Wine Only
SERVING: Dinner; closed Mondays
PRICE RANGE: $$
Chef Klime Kovaceski's Italian eatery specializes in pizza with gourmet toppings like figs, pesto-artichoke and fresh

basil. The creative menu offers a variety of Mediterranean dishes from chef Kovaceski's personal recipes. Delivery available.

DOLORES, BUT YOU CAN CALL ME LOLITA
1000 S. Miami Ave., Miami: 305-403-3103
www.doloreslolita.com
CUISINE: American
DRINKS: Full Bar
SERVING: Lunch / Dinner
Romantic setting (except when it's jammed on weekend nights). Try to get a table on the patio upstairs. Pappardelle with kobe beef Bolognese; filet mignon funghi. $$$

EDGE STEAK & BAR
Four Seasons Hotel, 1435 Brickell Ave, Miami, 305-381-3190
www.edgerestaurantmiami.com
CUISINE: Seafood/Steakhouse/American (New)
DRINKS: Full bar
SERVING: Dinner
PRICE RANGE: $$$
NEIGHBORHOOD: Brickell
Luxury steakhouse located in the Four Season Hotel so expect the best. Located on the 7th floor of the Four Season, this eatery offers a great dining experience. Menu picks include: Pork & Pistachio Terrine and Chicken Liver and Foie Gras Pâté. Great choice for brunch.

FOOQ'S
1035 N Miami Ave, Miami, 786-536-2749
www.fooqsmiami.com
CUISINE: Persian / American (New)
DRINKS: Beer & Wine Only
SERVING: Dinner Tues-Sun; Lunch on Sun; Closed Mon
PRICE RANGE: $$$

NEIGHBORHOOD: **Downtown**
Located in downtown Miami's "nightclub" district, this unique eatery offers American fare with a Persian twist. Favorites: Braised lamb; Khoresh (which is Persian stew) and Delmonico steak. Reservations recommended.

FRATELLI MILANO
213 SE 1st St., Miami: 305-373-2300
www.ristorantefratellimilano.com
CUISINE: Italian
DRINKS: Beer/Wine
SERVING: Lunch / Dinner; closed Sunday.
Bucatini san Babila, thick pasta with sweet Italian sausage, broccoli, garlic, pecorino cheese in a tomato sauce; Fettuccine Allo Scoglio, homemade fettuccine, sauteed shrimp, scallops, calamari and mussels in a white wine sauce; lobster ravioli; Fiocchi di Pera.
$$-$$$

GARCIA'S SEAFOOD GRILLE & FISH MARKET
398 NW N. River Dr., Miami: 305-375-0765
www.garciasseafoodgrill.com
CUISINE: Seafood
DRINKS: Full Bar
SERVING: Lunch / Dinner
Long a popular seafood eatery on the Miami River. Just concentrate on the seafood, seafood, seafood. During stone crab season, they usually have a 2-4-1 special on Friday. A friend of mine with a boat goes down almost every Friday during season to get them, tying up at the dock in front of this place. Makes for a great afternoon. (I'm not listing **Casablanca,** which is just next door, but, many people prefer it over Garcia's. Me? I can't really tell the difference. They're both excellent.) $$-$$$

GRAZIANO'S RESTAURANT BRICKELL
177 SW 7th St., Miami: 305 860-1426
http://www.grazianosgroup.com
CUISINE: Argentine
DRINKS: full bar
SERVING: B'fast / Lunch / Dinner
Argentine steak house. Top quality meats, as would be expected. There's a great bakery here, so you have to go through it to the restaurant behind. Pastas with chicken is good if you're not into meats. There are chips with truffle oil dribbled over them. Also the spinach gnocchi. They have an excellent selection of Malbecs here – ask them to suggest a reasonably priced one (don't let them give you one for more than $35) if you're not familiar with this rich, red Argentine wine. $$$

HARD ROCK CAFE
Bayside Marketplace
401 Biscayne Blvd., Miami: 305 377-3110
http://www.hardrock.com
CUISINE: American
DRINKS: Full Bar
SERVING: Lunch / Dinner
You know what to expect here. Nothing too different. Standard chain menu. Nice overlooking marina at Bayside. Indoor-outdoor. $$$

II GABBIANO
335 S. Biscayne Blvd., Miami: 305-373-0063
www.ilgabbianomia.com
CUISINE: Italian
DRINKS: Full Bar
SERVING: Lunch weekdays, noon to 3; dinner from 5; closed Sunday.
Where the Miami River meets the Bay, you'll find this super excellent Italian restaurant. Everything you've heard

about it is true: it may be the best Italian restaurant in all of Florida, one of the best in the country. (**Scarpetta** in the **Fontainebleau** is right up there with this.) Fried zucchini, gnocchi with gorgonzola, mushroom ravioli ($39), grilled calamari is excellent; alla Scarpariello; spaghetti alla carbonara; ricotta cheesecake. Whatever pennies you have, this place is worth the last one. $$$$$

KIKI ON THE RIVER
450 NW North River Dr, Miami, 786-502-3243
www.kikiontheriver.com
CUISINE: Greek/Mediterranean
DRINKS: Beer & Wine Only
SERVING: Full Bar
PRICE RANGE: $$$$
NEIGHBORHOOD: Downtown
Chic waterfront eatery on the Miami River offers a menu of traditional Greek cuisine and seafood. It's a big spot that they spent a fortune on, with wooden planks outside facing the river, where you can dock a boat if you have one. It's hot in the summer, even with the fans whirring all around you. There is an indoor dining room, but it's no fun compared to outside. Favorites: Grilled octopus and Grilled scallops. Great cocktails. Can get crowded on the weekends and when they turn up the music, it's hard to bear. (Tip: save a fortune by coming during the week for lunch when they have a very reasonably priced prix fixe.)

KOMODO
801 Brickell Ave, Miami, 305-534-2211
www.komodomiami.com
CUISINE: Chinese/Asian Fusion
DRINKS: Full bar
SERVING: Lunch/Dinner; Dinner only on Sat & Sun
PRICE RANGE: $$$$
NEIGHBORHOOD: Brickell

Upscale eatery offering a high-end menu of Southeastern Asian fare. Massive multi-level dining room with dining indoors and out. Family-style menu items include favorites like: Lobster Dynamite and Grilled Szechuan Beef.

LARGO BAR & GRILL
Bayside, 401 Biscayne Blvd., Miami 305-374-9706
www.largobarandgrill.com
WEBSITE DOWN AT PRESSTIME
CUISINE: American
DRINKS: Full Bar
SERVING: Lunch / Dinner
Avoid Hooters and the Hard Rock and opt for this if you're in the downtown "tourist trap" called Bayside. Buffalo chicken salad, Philly cheesesteak, Angus sliders, crab cake sandwich, seafood Alfredo, chicken parm, scampi over pasta. $$-$$$

LOS GAUCHITOS STEAKHOUSE
The Doubletree Grand
1717 N. Bayshore Dr., Miami: 305-377-3133
www.gauchitosteakhouse.com/
CUISINE: Argentine steakhouse
DRINKS: Full Bar
SERVING: Lunch / Dinner
It's OK, but if this is the kind of food you want, there are *many* other better places similarly priced. Keep reading. $$$

NAOE
661Brickell Key Dr, Miami, 305-947-6263
www.naoemiami.com
CUISINE: Seafood/Steakhouse/Live Raw Food
DRINKS: Beer & Wine Only
SERVING: Dinner
PRICE RANGE: $$$$

NEIGHBORHOOD: Brickell

Contemporary Japanese bistro offering a creative fixed-price (Omakase) menu. Note there's no sign on the front door so you must look for the number 661. Definitely a culinary experience for fans of sushi and the chef offers seconds of any piece of sushi served during your meal. Not for the budget diners. Reservations recommended.

NOVECENTO
1414 Brickell Ave.,Miami: 305-403-0900
www.novecento.com
CUISINE: Contemporary Argentine
DRINKS: Full Bar
SERVING: Lunch / Dinner
Not just steaks; excellent seafood as well. $$-$$$

NOVIKOV
300 S Biscayne Blvd, Miami, 305-489-1000
https://www.novikovmiami.com/
CUISINE: Chinese/Japanese/Seafood
DRINKS: Full bar

SERVING: Lunch and Dinner, Dinner only on Sat.
NEIGHBORHOOD: Downtown
PRICE RANGE: $$$$
Upscale world-renowned eatery (with outposts in London, Dubai, Tokyo) featuring a globally sourced menu of robata grill and wok dishes. The interior is sleek, modern, refreshing. Great display of fish on ice from all over the world. Extensive Dim Sum and Sushi selection. Favorites: Grilled Branzino scallion & ginger; Peking Duck is a specialty; Wagyu skirt steak and Salmon maki. (The corn on the cob side is excellent.) Vegan options. Delicious desserts. Outdoor seating.

PEGA GRILL
15 E. Flagler St., Miami: 305-808-6666
www.pegagrill.com
CUISINE: Greek
DRINKS: Beer/Wine
SERVING: Lunch
Nice spot for good Greek food that's fast and cheap. $$

RIVER OYSTER BAR
also known as **RIVER SEAFOOD & OYSTER BAR**
33 SE 7th St Suite 100, Miami: 305-530-1915
www.therivermiami.com
CUISINE: Seafood
DRINKS: Full Bar
SERVING: Lunch / Dinner
Though they have a substantial menu, I don't think I've sat at a table here in years. I always slither up to the bar and order a couple of dozen oysters mixed from the selection they currently have available. And have a bottle of wine or a couple of beers. $$$

RIVERWALK CAFE
Hyatt Regency Miami

400 SE 2nd Ave., Miami: 305 358-1234
www.hyatt.com/en-US/hotel/florida/hyatt-regency-miami/miarm/dining
CUISINE: American; some Latin
DRINKS: Full Bar
SERVING: B'fast / Lunch / Dinner
Typical hotel restaurant offering the expected American menu with a few "Latin" items thrown in to remind you that you're in Miami. Better than eating here, go outside and get the real thing. $$$

SOYA & POMODORO
120 NE 1st St., Miami: 305-381-9511
www.soyaepomodoro.com
CUISINE: Italian
DRINKS: Beer/Wine
SERVING: Lunch (weekdays); Dinner (Thursday-Saturday)
This charming little spot is located in the old Dupont Building, so you're immediately enclosed in an architectural style that will make you feel like you're in Europe. Food is good, cheap Italian, from the south. $-$$

SPARKY'S ROADSIDE RESTAURANT & BAR
204 NE 1st St., Miami: 305-377-2877
www.sparkysroadsidebarbecue.com
CUISINE: Barbeque
DRINKS: Beer/Wine
SERVING: Lunch / Dinner
BBQ in the dry-rubbed style. Very nice. They make their own sauces. $-$$

SUVICHE
49 SW 11th St., Miami: 305-960-7097
www.suviche.com
CUISINE: Sushi, Peruvian, Japanese
DRINKS: Beer/Wine
SERVING: Lunch / Dinner
Tiny, tiny place serving excellent Peruvian-Japanese food. $$

TORO TORO
Intercontinental
100 Chopin Plaza, Miami: 305-372-4710
www.torotoromiami.com
CUISINE: Latin American, Steakhouse, Tapas
DRINKS: Full Bar
SERVING: Lunch, Dinner
Authentic Latin American dishes in Miami's iconic InterContinental Hotel. Delicious menu items include dozens of tapas, flat bread pizza, and lamb anticuchos. Also grouper pan-roasted and a caldo de pollo. For lunch, get the pepito steak sandwich. $$$

TRULUCK'S SEAFOOD, STEAK & CRABHOUSE
777 Brickell Ave., Miami: 305-579-0035
www.trulucks.com
CUISINE: Seafood, Steakhouse

DRINKS: Full Bar
SERVING: Lunch (weekdays) /Dinner nightly
Most steakhouses offer big lobsters just because they can, but their hearts are with the steaks. Here, it's just the opposite. While you can get really great steaks, their hearts are with the seafood. (They catch their own stone crabs, and it's cheaper than Joe's). Fine menu complemented by very good service. $$$-$$$$

ZUMA
Epic Hotel
270 Biscayne Blvd. Way, Miami: 305 577-0277
http://www.zumarestaurant.com
CUISINE: Japanese
DRINKS: Full Bar
SERVING: Lunch (till 3); dinner from 6.
This rave-inducing spot will thrill you if you're into Japanese fine food. Lobster tempura, ribeye with wafu sauce, salmon teriyaki, grilled scallops, black cod, mushroom risotto. You'll love the view overlooking the docks and the River. $$$$

LITTLE HAVAVA

While there's a lot more to Little Havana than Cuban food, it's the Cuban food you come for.

ANTIGUA GUATEMALA CAFETERIA
2741 W Flagler St., Miami: 305-643-0304
No web site
CUISINE: Central American
DRINKS: Beer/ Wine
SERVING: B'fast / Lunch / Dinner

Although the name suggests differently, this eatery serves up mostly Central American dishes. Pupusas (corn tortillas stuffed with cheese, beans, chicharron, or a revuelto, a combination of all three), a variety of daily soups, stuffed peppers, pickled pork and churrasco. $

CASA JUANCHO
2436 SW 8th St., Miami: 305-642-2524
http://www.casajuancho.com
CUISINE: Spanish
DRINKS: Full Bar
SERVING: Lunch / Dinner
In this well-known eatery, Spanish delicacies include baby eel and hand carved ham from acorn fed Iberian pigs. $$$$

DON CAMARON SEAFOOD GRILL
501 NW 37 Ave., Miami: 305-642-6767
www.doncamaronrestaurant.com
CUISINE: Seafood
DRINKS: Beer/ Wine
SERVING: B'fast / Lunch / Dinner
Here you will find everything seafood; fish dishes come with rice and your choice of plantains or French fries. Get there early; this place fills up fast. $-$$

EL JACALITO TAQUERIA MEXICANA
3622 W Flagler St., Miami: 305-443-1336
www.jacalitomexicanrestaurant.com
CUISINE: Mexican
DRINKS: Beer/ Wine
SERVING: B'fast / Lunch / Dinner
You will feel right at home in this small and quaint restaurant. Although they serve up traditional Mexican dishes, it's the tacos that are a must have. Huge selection of tacos including tongue, cow cheek, cochinita pibil

(shredded pork), chorizo, beef, chicken, and vegetables. $-$$

EL PALACIO DE LOS JUGOS
5721 W Flagler St., Miami: 305-264-1503
www.elpalaciodelosjugos.com
SEVERAL LOCATIONS
CUISINE: Cuban
DRINKS: No Alcohol
SERVING: B'fast / Lunch / Dinner
This landmark is a one-stop shop including a market overflowing with fresh fruits and vegetables and a juice bar serving an array of juices and *batidos*. But their cafeteria style prepared foods you can get here is **some of the best Cuban food you can get in Miami,** not the usual Cuban greasy slop you find on most corners. $

LA CAMARONERA FISH MARKET
1952 W. Flagler St., Miami: 305-642-3322
http://garciabrothersseafood.com

CUISINE: Cuban Seafood
DRINKS: No Alcohol
SERVING: B'fast / Lunch / Dinner
No seats in this eatery, just a counter that you can lean on making this place a true Cuban fish-fry. Get there early, it fills up fast. $

LA CARRETA
3632 SW 8th St., Miami: 305-444-7501
http://www.lacarreta.com
CUISINE: Cuban
DRINKS: Full Bar
SERVING: B'fast / Lunch / Dinner
Although not the most gourmet of Cuban cuisine, it is a great place to get traditional dishes. Great daily specials. $$

LA CASITA CUBAN CUISINE
3805 SW 8th St., Miami: 305-448-8224
www.lasvegascubancuisine.com
CUISINE: Cuban
DRINKS: Full Bar
SERVING: Lunch / Dinner
Surprisingly low-key and mellow, this place serves up delicious typical Cuban dishes at affordable prices. $

LAS TAPAS DE ROSA
449 SW 8th St., Miami: 305-856-9788
www.tapasderosa.com
CUISINE: Spanish, Tapas
DRINKS: Beer & Wine
SERVING: Lunch, Dinner
This little family-run restaurant is known for serving some of the best tapas in Miami, almost all under $10. Old World feel, friendly service, and extensive Spanish wine list. $$

VERSAILLES
3555 SW 8th St., Miami: 305-444-0240
www.versaillesrestaurant.com
CUISINE: Cuban
DRINKS: Full Bar
SERVING: B'fast / Lunch / Dinner
A staple of the Cuban community, this is as authentic as it gets. Every politician, from mayor to president, comes by this place to woo the Cuban vote & drum up support. But I've never thought the food was *that* good. I've had much better Cuban food a dozen other places. The Cuban coffee is a must have, of course. $$

CORAL GABLES

Coral Gables has never been known for excitement. In fact, the city fathers are so aware of the city's image that they seek to control just about everything, from the size of a realtor's sign on a lawn to the color of a newspaper box on the corner.

But as dull as the Gables can be, one place where the excitement has always been at the uppermost level is in the field of fine dining.
Even with the explosion of great restaurants on South Beach (and more lately, Downtown), the swank eateries in the Gables have held their own, and make the "City Beautiful" really a "City Bountiful."

BRASSERIE CENTRAL
320 San Lorenzo Ave, Coral Gables, 786-536-9388
www.brasseriecentralmiami.com
CUISINE: French
DRINKS: Full Bar
SERVING: Dinner
PRICE RANGE: $$
NEIGHBORHOOD: Merrick Park/Coral Gables
Cute brasserie serving classic French fare with the atmosphere of a Parisian café. Menu picks: Saumon Fume Ecossais (smoked Salmon) and fresh Pate. Raw bar. Nice selection of wines and champagne.

BULLA GASTROBAR
2500 Ponce De Leon Blvd, Coral Gables, 786-810-6215
https://bullagastrobar.com/locations/coral-gables/
CUISINE: Spanish/Tapas Bar
DRINKS: Full Bar
SERVING: Lunch & Dinner
PRICE RANGE: $$
NEIGHBORHOOD: Coral Gables
Popular eatery serving Spanish and Catalan dishes. Favorites: Patatas Bravas and Huevos Bulla. Variety of tapas (more than 20) and daily specials.

CAFFE ABBRACCI
318 Aragon Ave., Coral Gables: 305-441-0700
http://www.caffeabbracci.com

CUSINE: Italian
DRINKS: Full Bar
SERVING: Lunch / Dinner
True to his native Venezia, owner Nino Pernetti continues his time-honored tradition of bringing quintessential classic Northern Italian dishes to his customers in this "power" lunch and dinner spot. A lot of big shots eat here, but Nino makes them pay for the privilege. Indoor-outdoor. $$$$

CANTON AND SUSHI MAKI
2614 Ponce de Leon Blvd., Coral Gables: 305-448-3736
http://www.cantonrestaurants.com
CUSINE: Sushi
DRINKS: Beer/Wine
SERVING: Lunch / Dinner
Good Chinese and sushi since 1975, specializing in generously portioned Chinese cuisine served family style for dine-in, take-out, delivery and catering. $$

CHRISTY'S
3101 Ponce de Leon Blvd., Coral Gables: 305-446-1400
http://www.christysrestaurant.com
CUSINE: Steakhouse
DRINKS: Full Bar
SERVING: Dinner
Diners at this Miami landmark restaurant enjoy the famous Caesar salad, aged Midwestern beef and the daily fresh Florida seafood. Impossible to go wrong here. $$$$

EATING HOUSE
Located in Cafe Ponce
804 Ponce De Leon Blvd, Coral Gables, 305-448-6524
www.eatinghousemiami.com
CUISINE: American (New)
DRINKS: Beer & Wine

SERVING: Lunch & Dinner, Lunch only on Sat; closed Mondays
PRICE RANGE: $$
NEIGHBORHOOD:
Small eatery serving a menu of locally sourced dishes. Menu picks: Pasta carbonara and Chicken & waffles. Usually busy with a wait. Reservations recommended.

FONTANA
The Biltmore
1200 Anastasia Ave., Coral Gables: 305-913-3200
http://www.biltmorehotel.com
CUSINE: Mediterranean

DRINKS: Full Bar
SERVING: B'fast / Lunch / Dinner
Enjoy authentic Italian cuisine in a casual brasserie featuring outdoor dining in a courtyard setting. Main reason to come here is to see the famous hotel. $$$$

FRATELLINO
264 Miracle Mile, Coral Gables, 786-452-0068
No Website
CUISINE: Italian
DRINKS: Beer & Wine Only
SERVING: Lunch/Dinner; Dinner-only on Sun
PRICE RANGE: $$
NEIGHBORHOOD: Coral Gables
Small intimate eatery offering delicious Italian fare. Menu picks include: Risotto alla Pescatora and Risotto alla Pescatora. Also a big favorite is the fried calamari & zucchini. Delicious tiramisu and cheesecake.

FRENCHIE'S DINER
2618 Galiano St, Coral Gables, 305-442-4554
www.frenchiesdiner.com
CUISINE: French
DRINKS: Beer & Wine
SERVING: Lunch & Dinner; closed Sun & Mon
PRICE RANGE: $$
NEIGHBORHOOD: Coral Gables
Friendly eatery offering typical diner fare along with creative daily specials. Favorites: Duck Club Sandwich and Risotto with wild mushrooms.

GRAZIANO'S
394 Giralda Ave., Coral Gables: 305-774 3599
http://www.grazianosgroup.com
CUSINE: Argentine Steakhouse
DRINKS: Full Bar

SERVING: Lunch / Dinner
This restaurant is a traditional Argentinean steakhouse. A nice experience for meat and wine lovers. Also pastas, salads and seafood. $$$

HILLSTONE RESTAURANT
201 Miracle Mile, Coral Gables, 305-529-0141
www.hillstone.com
CUISINE: American (New)/Sushi
DRINKS: Full bar
SERVING: Lunch/Dinner
PRICE RANGE: $$$
NEIGHBORHOOD: Coral Gables
Upscale restaurant offering a menu of steak, sushi, seafood, and pastas.
Upscale chain eatery featuring steak, seafood & pasta alongside specialty cocktails. Great meat sandwiches and amazing salads. Try their signature dessert tres leches with fresh fruit. Nice wine selection. Reservations a must on weekends.

LA PALMA RISTORANTE
116 Alhambra Circle, Coral Gables: 305 445-8777
http://www.lapalmaristorante.com
CUSINE: Italian
DRINKS: Full Bar
SERVING: Lunch / Dinner
Northern Italian cuisine. Located in a restored historic building. Tree-covered courtyard with its stone fountain is both relaxing and romantic. The inside dining room's fine art gives guests the feeling of dining in a gallery. Outdoor dining. $$$$

LIBERTY CAFFE
997 N. Greenway Drive, Coral Gables: 305-392-1211
http://www.libertycaffe.com

CUSINE: Italian
DRINKS: Beer/Wine
SERVING: B'fast / Lunch / Dinner
This is the ideal neighborhood spot for a morning coffee or a cool gelato on a warm afternoon. House-made gelatos, pressed sandwiches, oven-baked pizza breads, specialty coffees and espresso. $$

MESAMAR
264 Giralda Ave, Coral Gables, 305-640-8448
www.mesamar.com
CUISINE: Seafood
DRINKS: Full bar
SERVING: Lunch & Dinner
PRICE RANGE: $$$$
MesaMar serves delicious seafood fusion with an Oriental influence. Favorites include: Tuna & lobster tacos and Calamari.

MORTON'S THE STEAKHOUSE
2333 Ponce De Leon Blvd., Coral Gables: 305 442-1662
http://www.mortons.com/coralgables
CUSINE: Steakhouse
DRINKS: Full Bar
SERVING: Lunch / Dinner
For more than 30 years this restaurant has served the finest quality food, featuring USDA prime-aged beef, fresh fish and seafood, big salads, delicious appetizers and elegant desserts. Indoor-outdoor. $$$$

PASCAL'S ON PONCE
2611 Ponce De Leon Blvd, Coral Gables, 305-444-2024
www.pascalmiami.com
CUISINE: French
DRINKS: Full Bar

SERVING: Lunch & Dinner, Dinner only on Sat; closed on Sundays
PRICE RANGE: $$$$
NEIGHBORHOOD: Coral Gables
Cozy bistro serving modern French fare. Favorites: Scallops and Crab cakes. Nice dessert selection. Impressive wine selection. Upscale dining experience.

RED FISH GRILL
9610 Old Cutler Road, Miami: 305- 668-8788
http://www.redfishgrill.net
CUSINE: Seafood
DRINKS: Beer/Wine
SERVING: Dinner
Located on the shore of Biscayne Bay in Matheson Hammock Park, this restaurant is a breath of fresh air at the water's edge. Get the pan-fried snapper ($30). The main treat here is the "old Florida" setting. Indoor-outdoor. $$$

RED KOI THAI & SUSHI LOUNGE
317 Miracle Mile, Coral Gables: 305- 446-2690

http://www.redkoilounge.com
CUSINE: Sushi/Thai
DRINKS: Full Bar
SERVING: Dinner
Asian fusion. Indoor-outdoor. $$$

RINCON ARGENTINO
2345 SW 37th Ave., Coral Gables: 305- 444-2494
http://www.rinconargentino.com
CUSINE: Latin/American
DRINKS: Full Bar
SERVING: Lunch / Dinner
Fine meats and homemade pastas in this Argentine eatery. $$$

SAWA
Village of Merrick Park
360 San Lorenzo Ave., Coral Gables: 305-447-6555
http://www.sawarestaurant.com
CUSINE: Mediterranean
DRINKS: Full Bar
SERVING: Lunch / Dinner
Mediterranean and Japanese cuisines. (Huh?) Chef Jouvens Jean merges an innovative sushi menu with a memorable ensemble of tapas and entrees. Inside there are white walls, white chandeliers, white leather upholstery, vividly colorful interactive 3D artworks by Chady Elias, and an LED light show behind the bar. On the patio, there are billowing white curtains and white leather sofas, where guests can puff away on flavored Hookahs. (Well…) $$$$

SEASONS 52
321 Miracle Mile, Coral Gables: 305- 442-8552
http://www.seasons52.com
CUSINE: American
DRINKS: Full Bar

SERVING: Lunch / Dinner
Comfy grill and wine bar always seems to have a youngish, attractive crowd and the bar scene is fun, too. They emphasize fresh ingredients. (The flatbreads here can feed two, and they're cheap, cheap, cheap!) $$-$$$

THREEFOLD CAFÉ
141 Giralda Ave, Coral Gables, 305-704-8007
www.threefoldcafe.com
CUISINE: Australian/Cafe
DRINKS: Full bar
SERVING: Breakfast & Lunch; Dinner on Thur, Fri & Sat
PRICE RANGE: $$
NEIGHBORHOOD: Downtown
Great choice for a gourmet breakfast or brunch serving top notch coffee and creative breakfast treats. Delicious breads, benedicts, and French toast. Fresh juices and homemade breads.

TWO SISTERS RESTAURANT
Hyatt Regency
50 Alhambra Plaza, Coral Gables: 305- 441-1234
https://coralgables.regency.hyatt.com/en/hotel/dining/TwoSistersRestaurant.html
CUSINE: French/Greek/Mediterranean
DRINKS: Full Bar
SERVING: B'fast / Lunch / Dinner
With the wide variety of things going on with this menu, they should have named it **Four Sisters Who Can't Make Up Their Mind!** $$$

XIXON SPANISH RESTAURANT
2101 Coral Way, Miami, 305-854-9350
www.xixonspanishrestaurant.com **WEBSITE DOWN AT PRESSTIME**
CUISINE: Spanish/Tapas Bar

DRINKS: Full Bar
SERVING: Lunch & Dinner
PRICE RANGE: $$
NEIGHBORHOOD: Shenandoah
This modern multi-level Spanish eatery featuring several rooms—a dining room, wine cellar and bakery/deli—is one of my favorite spots in the Gables. The bakery/deli & market give it a bustling feel most restaurants would die for. Food is uniformly outstanding. Large menu. Favorites: Seafood paella and Manchego. Lots of great dishes to share like fried artichokes and octopus. They get the cod from the chilly waters off Iceland.

COCONUT GROVE

While the days of Coconut Grove's ascendency in Miami is just a faded memory, there still are a few restaurants nice enough to warrant a visit.

ARIETE
3540 Main Hwy, Coconut Grove, 786-615-3747
https://arietecoconutgrove.com/
CUISINE: American (New)
DRINKS: Full Bar
SERVING: Dinner Tues – Sun, Lunch Sat & Sun; closed Monday
PRICE RANGE: $$$
NEIGHBORHOOD: Coconut Grove
Modern farmhouse décor (snugly arranged wooden tables) with a bar on one side of the room and an open kitchen and a wood-burning oven on the other with an ever-changing menu of American fare. Favorites: Grilled oysters, Short rib and Venison. The small plates are really small. (Too small.) By way of contrast, the Painted Hills rib eye fills the whole plate and can feed 3. Great place for weekend

brunch (if you don't mind spotty service). Classic cocktails. Music tends to be intrusively loud.

CHUG'S

3444 Main Hwy Suite 21, Coconut Grove, 786-534-8722
www.chugsdiner.com
CUISINE: Cuban Diner
DRINKS: Beer & Wine
SERVING: Breakfast, Lunch, and Dinner
PRICE RANGE: $
Authentic Cuban eatery serving favorites like Short Rib Croquets, Pan con Lechon and of course Café con leche. Plenty of outdoor seating. Wow! Someplace cheap to eat in the Grove.

EL CARAJO

2465 SW 17th Ave., Miami: 305 856-2424
http://www.el-carajo.com
CUISINE: Spanish; tapas.
DRINKS: beer/wine.
SERVING: lunch, dinner daily.
Huge wine selection (1500 in stock). Small place, seats only 55, but good, solid food. $-$$.

GLASS AND VINE

2820 McFarlane Rd, Coconut Grove, 305-200-5268
www.glassandvine.com
CUISINE: American (New)
DRINKS: Full Bar
SERVING: Lunch & Dinner
PRICE RANGE: $$
NEIGHBORHOOD: Coconut Grove
Located within Peacock Park, this indoor/outdoor eatery offers an impressive Euro-style menu.
Favorites: Watermelon salad, Skewered broccoli and Scallops, roasted lamb ribs. I'm a big fan of the iceberg

wedge. But here, they take whole baby heads of Romaine and grill them with charred tomato, bacon, buttermilk and blue cheese—little bits of buckwheat replace traditional croutons. Outstanding! Intimate garden offers a great dining experience.

JAGUAR CEVICHE SPOON BAR & LATAM GRILL
3067 Grand Ave, Coconut Grove: 305 444-0216
https://jaguarrestaurant.com/
CUISINE: Latin.
DRINKS: full bar.
SERVING: lunch, dinner daily.
Ceviches served in large white ceramic spoons. Try something different: *chiles en nogada*, which is a dish made with poblano peppers jammed with pork and covered in a walnut-cream sauce. The Latam Grill has grilled steaks and seafood. All very nice. The meats are paired with distinctive Latin salsas. Indoor, outdoor. Casual. $$$-$$$$

LOCAL
3190 Commodore Plaza, Miami, 305-442-3377
www.lokalmiami.com
CUISINE: Burgers/American (New)
DRINKS: Beer & Wine
SERVING: Lunch and Dinner
PRICE RANGE: $$
Casual laid-back eatery offering a menu of burgers, sandwiches and beer. (Menu items are made with local, sustainable ingredients.) It's a little nicer than a dive, which it would have to be in this location in the heart of the Grove. You have to sell a lot of craft beer to pay the rents on this street. Favorites: Steak Sandwich and "My Childhood Dream" burger (their specialty).

LULU
3105 Commodore Plaza, Coconut Grove: 305 447-5858
http://www.luluinthegrove.com
CUISINE: Hard to pin down.
DRINKS: full bar.
SERVING: lunch, dinner daily.
Although the menu is all over the place, it's basically an American menu with a few things (like churrasco and some pastas) thrown in to give it some variety. Nice, cozy spot right in the heart of the Grove. $$$

MONTY'S RAW BAR
2550 S. Bayshore Dr., Coconut Grove: 305-856-3992
www.montysrawbar.com
CUISINE: American.
DRINKS: full bar.
SERVING: lunch, dinner.
This joint has been here forever. Back when the Grove was "the" place to be, it was one of the hottest tickets in town. Still offers casual waterfront indoor and outdoor dining. Seafood, sandwiches, salads and ribs while listening to live music and sitting on Biscayne Bay. $$$

TIGERTAIL + MARY
3321 Mary St, Coconut Grove, 305-722-5688
https://tigertailandmary.com
CUISINE: American (New)
DRINKS: Full bar
SERVING: Lunch and Dinner, Brunch
PRICE RANGE: $$$
Upscale neighborhood eatery here in the Grove with a clean, modern simple décor. I love the plants hanging from the shelves behind the bar, mixed in with bowls and bottles and jars Features a menu of American fare. Favorites: Tuna Crudo and Grilled Octopus. Indoor/Outdoor seating. Popular Brunch destination. Daily Happy Hour 5-7 p.m.

KEY BISCAYNE

If you find yourself on the Key, as we call it here in Miami, you could do worse than to drop into one of these nice eateries.

EL GRAN INKA
606 Crandon Blvd., Key Biscayne: 305 365-7883
http://www.graninka.com
CUISINE: Peruvian.
DRINKS: full bar.
SERVING: lunch, dinner.
You'd never know this was a chain (they have outlets in Guatemala, El Salvador, Costa Rica, but in the USA, they are only in Miami in 3 locations). Really good Peruvian food. This is an upscale place, but there are other places you can get great Peruvian food (see **Chalon's** on South Beach) for a quarter the price point. $$$$

LIGHTHOUSE CAFÉ
1200 Crandon Blvd., Key Biscayne, 305-361-8487
www.lighthouserestaurants.com
CUISINE: Cafes
DRINKS: No Booze

SERVING: Breakfast-Lunch
PRICE RANGE: $$
NEIGHBORHOOD: Key Biscayne
Completely open-air eatery in Bill Bagg's Cape Florida State Park, so make sure the weather's to your liking. Has a large menu, salads, sandwiches, pastas and some Cuban dishes (like pork chunks and black bean soup).There's a small fee to enter the park.

NOVECENTO
620 Crandon Blvd., Key Biscayne: 305 362-0900
http://www.novecento.com
CUISINE: Argentine steakhouse.
DRINKS: full bar.
SERVING: lunch, dinner.
Although to me this is basically an Argentine steakhouse (and it's really good), they say it's not just Argentine, but also Mediterranean and Pan Latin highlighted by French techniques. That the cuisine is not a fusion; rather each style is separate and is a pure reflection of its heritage. But to me, it's still an Argentine steakhouse. Indoor, outdoor.

RUSTY PELICAN
3201 Rickenbacker Causeway, Key Biscayne: 305 361-3818
www.therustypelican.com
CUISINE: American; seafood.
DRINKS: full bar.
SERVING: lunch, dinner daily.
Heavy on the seafood dishes, but what you really come here for is the spectacular view of downtown Miami. It's got an off-putting "corporate" feel to it and is huge (seats 400, but can do parties for 1,000). I always go on "off" days, and wouldn't be caught dead here on a Friday or Saturday night. But I know many people who love it when it's jammed. It's great for either lunch or dinner, depending on whether you want to look at the view in sunny daylight or romantic evenings. I even like it here on rainy, gusty days because I like looking out over the water when it's stormy. $$$

WHISKEY JOE'S BAR & GRILL
3301 Rickenbacker Cswy., Key Biscayne: 305-423-6590
www.whiskeyjoestampa.com/
CUISINE: American

DRINKS: Full Bar
SERVING: Lunch, Dinner
An offshoot of the original Tampa bar & grill, this location has a Key West vibe serving everything from crab cake sliders to mango salad with coconut shrimp. Live music.
$$

NIGHTLIFE

SOUTH BEACH
HOTEL LOBBY BARS - NIGHTCLUBS – BARS & LOUNGES - DIVES – GAY BARS & CLUBS

THE MAINLAND
NIGHTCLUBS - MAINLAND
BARS & LOUNGES – MAINLAND

***

SOUTH BEACH

A night on the town means different things to different people: some people want to go to a nightclub, spend $300 for bottle service. For someone else, it's a stroll on the beach.

HOTEL LOBBY BARS

Most tourists usually only see the lobby of the hotel they're in. Unless a nightclub or lounge (like **Wall** in the **W**) is located in a hotel, they don't see other hotel lobbies.

Or—more to the point here—the bars in or off the lobbies that can be worth a trip in and of themselves.

One of the things I like to do when I'm entertaining out-of-towners is to take them on a **Hotel Lobby Bar Tour**. The idea is simple: select a list of four or five or six hotels and spend the evening moving from one to the other. Have a single drink in each, maybe an appetizer or two if you're peckish, and then get out and go on to the next one. You'll have had one of the best evenings of your visit. And you'll absorb quite a visual education on the glories of architectural design on South Beach—all for the (sometimes hefty) price of a drink.

It's essential to appreciate what the South Beach lobby bars are like (for comparison's sake) to make a short excursion (a ten-minute Uber / Lyft ride) up to the **Eden Roc** and the **Fontainebleau**, hotels next door to each other, both designed by the legendary architect **Morris Lapidus**, the man who once said, "Too much is never enough."

Walk through the lobby of the Fontainebleau first. It's quite expansive. Have a drink and then walk next door to the Eden Roc. These lobbies are stunning.

Then come back to South Beach and see what other designers have done to fully appreciate the over-the-top genius of Morris Lapidus.

MONDRIAN
1100 West Ave., Miami Beach: 305-514-1500
www.mondrian-miami.com
Here you'll get a full sense of how strong Starck's influence is. Here it's all white, white and whiter. There's a stunning indoor bar, and this as well as the restaurant overlook the pool and Biscayne Bay. Outdoor bar as well. This is "Sunset Central," as it's the only hotel besides the Standard that faces west.

THE SAGAMORE
1671 Collins Ave., Miami Beach: 305-535-8088
www.sagamoresouthbeach.com
With 93 suites and two-story bungalows, the Sagamore is a bit big for a "boutique" hotel (though to be fair it does possess a boutique hotel's attention to service and detail). Not in question, however, is the inn's designation as an "Art Hotel."

THE SETAI
2001 Collins Ave., Miami Beach: 305-520-6000
www.thesetaihotel.com
The front half of this uber luxury inn is the '30s era Dempsey Vanderbilt Hotel; the remainder is a modern glass tower that reaches up past the imagination. When you enter the lobby bar in this place you leave South Beach behind and move into a whole other dimension.

W SOUTH BEACH
2201 Collins Ave., Miami Beach: 305-938-3000
www.wsouthbeach.com

The Living Room Bar off the lobby will give you an idea of what the big money buys in terms of design today. Expect this place to be busy, because it's the Hot Spot this year. If you're going for dinner, let the trendsetters trip over themselves at **Mr. Chow** while you go to **Solea**, one of the best true Spanish restaurants in town. Also home to the uber-hip bottle club lounge, **Wall**.

THE VICTOR
1144 Ocean Dr., Miami Beach: 305-779-8700
www.hotelvictorsouthbeach.com
If you must hit Ocean Drive, then this is the place. Designed by the famed L. Murray Dixon in 1937 and retrofit by Parisian Jacques Garcia back in 2003 (to the reported tune of $48 million), the Victor's got both a charming lobby bar (V Bar) and a beautiful pool-with-a-view (Vue). And if you close your eyes you're on a classic ocean liner, and South Beach is as wondrous as ever. Take special note of the restored mural in the lobby.

NIGHTCLUBS

BASEMENT
2901 Collins Ave, Miami Beach, 786-257-4600
www.basementmiami.com
Located in the basement of **The Edition**, one of Miami Beach's hottest new hotels just a tad bit north of South Beach, this unique club was developed by Ian Schrager of Studio 54 offering music from Miami veteran Ben Pundole. A gathering spot for hipsters and those who aspire to be cool. Dress the part.

BODEGA TAQUERIA Y TEQUILA
1220 16th St, Miami Beach, 305-704-2145
www.bodegataqueria.com/
Some come for the great Mexican street food (I come here with a Mexican who says the tacos are the best) but others come for the great bar scene located behind the door that looks like it leads to a port-a-potty. It actually leads down a short hallway to one of the hippest bars in Miami. This bar offers a relaxed atmosphere with friendly bartenders (a rarity these days) serving creative cocktails. Velvet couches, unique art, and a chill balcony. Pool table, DJs, and rowdy crowd, most of them with more tattoos than I care to see, but the place is happening. I take visitors here, but it's not a place for an old fart like me to hang out.

LIV
Fontainebleau, 4441 Collins Ave., Miami Beach: 305-674-4680
www.livnightclub.com/
The Fontainebleau's signature hotspot may need no introduction, especially if you're familiar with the likes of **Tiesto** and **Cedric Gervais**. But wall-to-wall weekends of world-class DJs is only one of the reasons to trek up

Collins and join the madding crowd; the other is Wednesday night's **Dirty Harry** party, which pits Miami's best spinners with some of the world's most out-there performers. Sure, it'll cost you. But some wild nights are well worth paying for.

NIKKI BEACH CLUB
1 Ocean Dr., Miami Beach: 305-538-1111
www.nikkibeach.com
What started out here at the foot of Ocean Drive now has outposts in places like Cabo San Lucas, Marbella, Cannes and all around the world. Full list of activities, but it's still a great place to lounge in the sun or play at night. And you're right on the beach, perfect for that nighttime walk with a moon over Miami. Dancing.

STORY
136 Collins Ave., Miami Beach: 305-479-4426
www.storymiami.com
I remember very well the nightclub Amnesia that once occupied this enormous space. Three levels of madness, all of it driven by heart-thumping music. Another outpost where $20 buys you a vodka cran.

BARS & LOUNGES

B BAR
1440 Ocean Dr., Miami Beach: 305-531-6100
www.thebetsyhotel.com
Designed by Chi-town power broker **Callin Fortis**, of Big Time Design Studios, the very same cat who brought the wild world everything Crobar to Exit 66, B Bar is the Betsy's basement playroom par excellence. And at equal parts speakeasy and hide-out, it's one of the damn few good reasons even to dare Ocean Drive anymore.

BROKEN SHAKER
Freehand Hotel, 2727 Indian Creek Dr, Miami Beach, 305-531-2727
www.thefreehand.com
Located in the backyard of the Freehand Hotel, formerly the Indian Creek Hotel, that has now been transformed into a hostel. Here you'll find the hostel's pool, herb garden, bocce ball court, ping pong tables and outdoor seating area. The crowd is friendly and there's often live music. Small menu available.

THE CATALINA HOTEL & BEACH CLUB
1732 Collins Ave., Miami Beach: 305-674-1160
www.catalinasouthbeach.com.
Over the past couple years the Catalina has turned into a sorta adult amusement park in its own right. There are the joints: **Maxine's Bistro**, **Kung Fu Kitchen** and **Sushi, Red Bar**. There are the pools: Bamboo and Rooftop. And then there's the Bridge – now Verge – Art Fair, which takes place each year at **Art Basel**. All in all, it's a

charming antidote to the mega-inns. And downright affordable to boot.

KILL YOUR IDOL

222 Espanola Way, Miami Beach: 305-672-1852
www.killyouridol.com **WEBSITE DOWN AT PRESSTIME**

Packed with pop culture artifacts such as a Playboy pinball machine and a life-sized Bruce Lee, this sleek little hang would be just what the locals ordered if she or he had any say in the matter. Drinks are less than cheap, and if you're hungry you can even grab food from The Alibi. And don't forget to drop a dime in that jukebox. DJ Smeejay is often seen bouncing the club in late hours.

LIVING ROOM - W HOTEL

2201 Collins Ave, Miami Beach, 305-938-3000
www.wsouthbeach.com/living-room-bar

Located in the lobby of W Hotel South Beach, this bar specializes in custom made cocktails filled with natural ingredients like fruits, herbs, & edible flowers. The drink menu features infused, molecular mixology, and innovative concoctions like the Electric Watermelon (made with fresh watermelon, rosemary honey, peach bitters, and bourbon then topped with honeydew caviar). Drinks are pricey.

MOKAI

235 - 23rd St., Miami Beach: 786-735-3322
www.mokaimiami.com/

Now owned by The Opium Group, Mokai still retains some of its storied hedonism. It just has a different accent.

MYNT

1921 Collins Ave., Miami Beach: 305-532-0727
www.myntlounge.com

Hot club serving locals and an international clientele. Big stars come here: Mickey Rourke, Sean Penn, Jennifer Lopez, Cameron Diaz, Britney Spears, Ricky Martin, Jamie Foxx, Colin Farrell.

SKYBAR
Shore Club
1901 Collins Ave., Miami Beach: 305-695-3100
www.shoreclub.com
Out by the pool you'll find the still-hot Skybar. Lots of celebs and heavy lifters.

DIVE BARS

Well, there used to be a lot more of *these* (does anyone remember **Jessie's Dollhouse Bar** on Washington Avenue?), but gentrification and soaring rents have squeezed a lot of colorful joints out of business. But a few remain.

MAC'S CLUB DEUCE
222 14th St. (between Collins & Washington), Miami Beach: 305-531-6200

www.macsclubdeuce.com/
The legendary dive bar where many scenes in "Miami Vice" were shot. The neon the crew put in was so cool owner **Mac Klein** left it up. (Mac celebrated his 100th birthday in 2015 and I was there. He died a year later at 101.) In this dive, which his family still operates the way Mac did, Happy Hour starts at 8 (ahem, that's 8 a.m., and runs till 7 p.m.). Regular patron "Persian Jimmy" used to say: "If you can't get drunk in eleven hours, you're not tryin'." A must visit. Buy a T-shirt.

FINNEGAN'S ROAD
942 Lincoln Rd., Miami Beach: 305-538-7997
https://finnegansroad.com/
Sports bar with lots of TVs. Pub fare. Low prices. The only real dive bar on Lincoln Road. ☹
I used to think the food here was awful, but I got stuck there one night in the rain and the chicken wings and French fries were to die for!

TED'S HIDEAWAY
124 Second St., Miami Beach: 305-532-9869
https://tedshideaway.net/
This dive bar has somehow managed not only to survive, but thrive in the high-end SoFi area where $20 million condos are not uncommon. It's a mere block from Prime 112 where steaks run over $100. But it's still here, where you can find pool tables, beer and booze and girl bartenders from places like Romania, Russia, Bulgaria. The owner's drinks aren't as skimpy as the outfits he makes the girls wear. By the way, the bar grub is pretty tasty, and cheap. A little seedier than the **Deuce**, and a little shadier too. So what? Open daily 8am-5am. Happy Hour starts at noon! One of my favorites.

Gone are the days when the big gay clubs provided that indefinable spark that ignited the South Beach nightlife scene and made it explode. The best "gay" clubs (**Warsaw Ballroom**—it ran from 1989 to 1998 and **Paragon**, from March 1992 to 1994, attracted a heady mix of gay *and* straight people, but they were all people "on the edge," at the forefront of whatever was happening. Add to this mix that the White Party was the first and most lavish party among the international gay **Circuit parties**, and you had a combustible environment.

It's waaaay different now. The cover at the Warsaw was $5. There was a tiny VIP Room upstairs. But mostly anybody could get into it. Money didn't matter. No bottle service. No attitude.

The reputation that South Beach is a huge gay Mecca lingers on and can't be shaken. But there's actually only a handful of gay bars on South Beach.

GAYTHERING
1409 Lincoln Rd, Miami Beach, 786-284-1176

www.gaythering.com
This bar is located in the cozy lobby of Miami Beach's only "straight friendly" hotel. Located where trendy Lincoln Road meets Biscayne Bay. It's a sleek bar with a friendly staff, craft cocktails, upscale ambience.

TWIST
1057 Washington Ave., Miami Beach: 305-538-9478.
www.twistsobe.com/
South Beach's famous long-running gay bar, where everybody goes after 3 a.m. to revel in what's left of the old decadence. (This is where the staffs of the other gays bars end up between 3 and 5 a.m.) They might have called this place the Last Chance Saloon because if you can't pick up someone here, you're really not trying very hard.

THE MAINLAND

NIGHTCLUBS MAINLAND

CHURCHILL'S PUB
5501 NE 2nd Ave., Miami: 305-757-1807
http://churchillspub.com
Up in Little Haiti, this joint (and it *is* a joint) offers live underground music. Been here since 1979. Indie music is the scene here.

EL PALENQUE NIGHTCLUB
1115 NW 22nd Ave., Miami: 305-644-7376
No web site at presstime
Well-known Mexican bands featured monthly. Other weekends, DJ Turko mans the turntables, playing bachata, salsa, and merengue on Fridays, open format on Saturdays,

and primarily Mexican music on Sundays. Nightly, a sexy dance contest. Patrons vote on the girl with the best presentation. Also bar food. Sometimes a cover, depending on entertainment.

SPACE
34 NE 11th St., Miami: 786-357-6456
http://clubspace.com
Big-time DJs and dancing is the scene here in this massive club. For the hard-partying set. Make sure your girlfriend doesn't get kidnapped and sold into slavery when everybody's so drunk they won't notice.

BARS & LOUNGES

THE ANDERSON MIAMI
709 NE 79th St., Miami, 786-401-6330
www.theandersonmiami.com
Located right off Biscayne Blvd, this hipster hangout (formerly Magnum's) is a combination of indoor and outdoor areas. The inside features a long dark bar area with great music and even a menu of snacks (from Fried chicken sandwich to TexMex). This new interpretation of an old theme offers a cleaner, hipper party atmosphere but the piano and dance floor remain.

THE BAR AT LEVEL 25
Conrad Hotel
1395 Brickell Ave., Miami - 305-503-6561
http://conradhotels1.hilton.com
Level 25 indicates that this bar is on the 25th floor, and worth a trip just to get a gander at the stunning view from this height. Best time to go is weekday happy-hour when prices drop to a reasonable $5 to $8. Later, prices go way up. Free valet parking (at least). Food served all day and

night. (Try the tempura-battered soft-shell crab with spicy chipotle aioli.)

BLUE MARTINI

900 S Miami Ave #250, Miami - 305-981-2583

http://bluemartinilounge.com

42 versions of the martini. This spot fills up with yuppies from nearby Brickell Avenue offices, but still a good-looking crowd. No one here didn't go to college. The servers are young and attractive, the bar food better than average. In Mary Brickell Village downtown. Happy hour specials; cover charge (if you can believe it) Friday and Saturday nights.

CHURCHILL'S PUB

5501 NE 2nd Ave., Miami: 305-757-1807

www.churchillspub.com

Place in Little Haiti that was here (from 1979) *before* there was a Little Haiti. Little Haiti just sort of grew up around Churchill's. I always find it funny to go over here, walk into the place, and find *white* people. Big supporter of the indie music scene, punk rock, etc.

THE CORNER

1035 N Miami Ave, Miami, 305-961-7887

www.thecornermiami.com/

Located in downtown's entertainment district (next door to Club Space), this charming nightspot offers a variety of interesting cocktails that you won't find next door. Here you'll find a modern-day saloon atmosphere and cocktails served with natural ingredients. This bar also boasts a nice selection of craft beers on draft, a price-conscious wine list and an impressive late-night menu.

EL PATIO WYNWOOD

167 NW 23 St, Miami, 786-409-2241

www.elpatiowynwood.com
Outdoor spot that is definitely part of the scene. Great specials (4 beers for $4? Bring it on). Lots of seating but it's all outdoors. Some of it is covered – some not. Nice selection of beers and crafted cocktails. Variety of tunes play depending on the DJ. Live bands usually play Latin music.

VAGABOND HOTEL LOUNGE/BAR
7301 Biscayne Blvd, Miami, 305-400-8420
www.thevagabondhotelmiami.com
Step back in time at relive the old Miami experience at the reopened Vagabond Hotel. This is one of my favorite spots in Miami. Lounge by the poolside bar – a mix of vintage Miami and Palm Springs. Great happy hour on weekends and affordable cocktails. (The restaurant is really good, too.)

INDEX

N

O

P

R

S

T

U

V

W

X

Z

When was the last time you had a dental check up ?

www.ingramcontent.com/pod-product-compliance
Ingram Content Group UK Ltd.
Pitfield, Milton Keynes, MK11 3LW, UK
UKHW021931200726
13853UKWH00010B/137